To Dot
Thank you for your
Support with atter
(in spirit).
Best wishes
Sarah.

Up Above The Streets and Houses

The origin of the street names of Houghton Regis

By Sarah Gelsthorp

Proceeds from the sale of this publication will be distributed to Houghton Regis charities or organisations.

Dedicated to my wonderful family who have encouraged me with the writing of this book, to my husband Martin, and our beautiful daughter Aimée (keep on writing!).

Sarah Gelsthorp asserts the right to be identified as the author of this work in accordance with the Copyright, Designs and Patents Act 1988.

Front and rear covers designed by Sarah Gelsthorp using photographs taken by the author (SEG).

Published by Sarah Gelsthorp,© September 2015.

ISBN 978-0-9933932-0-4

Printed in Great Britain by:
Catford Print Centre
3 Bellingham Road
London
SE6 2PN

CONTENTS

Left-
The Town Sign 2011
(SEG).

UP ABOVE THE STREETS AND HOUSES

Above-
The new Town Sign outside opposite the main Village Green February 2011 (SEG).

Houghton Regis is a small town in the Central Bedfordshire area with approx. 7500 properties, and 18,000 residents. The area has evolved in the last 60 years, from a small village, to a modern town, possessing industry, recreational facilities and popular community events.

It is known that Puddlehill (where Chalk Hill is now situated) was occupied from Neolithic times. Before Watling Street (now the A5) was cut through the chalk, Puddlehill and Maidenbower were on the same piece of downland. The hamlets of Puddlehill, Sewell, Bidwell and Thorn formed part of the parish of Houghton Regis, and are still recorded as such today. England was the subject of many invasions in earlier times, and, in 878 AD, there were raids by the Danes, leading to England being divided. Houghton Regis was in the middle of the two sides, and Anglo Saxon chronicles record an occasion in 913 AD, when the Danes set out to raid Luton. Thanks to local people, the aggressors were driven away, and by the time Edward the Confessor came to power in 1046, this was a peaceful land once more.

In the history books references to Houghton Regis have been found at the time of Edward the Confessor. In 1086, it was entered into the Domesday Book, which was a record of a survey of the land of England, carried out by the commissioners of

William 1st. The name of 'Houstone' was recorded in the Domesday Book, but many different versions of the name were recorded between the years of 1086 and 1353. The village name was recorded as Kyngshouton in 1287, while the name of Houghton Regis as seen today, was first used in 1353, with the suffix 'Regis' meaning 'Royal Manor'. It has also been thought that the name Houghton was of Saxon origin, with "Hoe" meaning spur of a hill, and "Tun" meaning village. Another name associated with the town is 'Saelig Houghton' ('saelig' meaning 'fortunate').

The oldest known building, which is standing in Houghton today, is the magnificent All Saints Parish Church, which was built in the $13^{th}/14^{th}$ century; possibly by the Sewell family (of the hamlet Sewell). Before this a Saxon Church stood on the same site, and is mentioned in the Domesday Book. Houghton Regis is also famous for Houghton Hall, the beautiful Village Green (at almost 7 acres) and Houghton Hall Park. There are also other listed buildings which once formed part of the original village. The Crown Inn, situated along East End, is another part of local history that is still appreciated today. The inn is on a register of alehouse licences of 1822, and is possibly the same building, which appears on a parish valuation of 1797.

The local boundary lines have been the subject of many changes, with much land being taken away from the Parish of Houghton Regis. The area today known as High Street North was formerly part of Upper Houghton, and was added to Dunstable in 1907. In April 1933, a few local streets underwent a name change, during the extension of the borough of Dunstable, and Poynters Road, Dunstable, which leads into Houghton Regis, was one of those streets. It was originally known as Park Road South, whilst Park Road North has still retained its original name.

Redevelopment of the area took place extensively from the late 1950s, with the Tithe Farm development and subsequently in the 1970s, when the Parkside Estate was built. Such redevelopment has to some extent continued ever since.

Houghton Regis officially became a town in January 1980 (hence its change from Parish Council to Town Council). At the time, the area didn't have its own badge or logo, and the newly formed Town Council set about having its own logo created, to be used on the Chain of Office for the Town Mayor. This badge is widely used today and includes All Saints Parish Church, the colour green, the cogs and the wheat sheaf to signify the agricultural and manufacturing nature of the area. In 2011 the Town Council erected a new place sign outside the Memorial Hall depicting many elements of the town's history.

Houghton Regis has evolved and changed, and it is set to change again within the very near future, with housing, retail and road networks. With every brick that is laid, we are writing the history of tomorrow.

Adapted from the Houghton Regis Town Guides, first published in 2005, and written by the author. Reproduced by kind permission of Houghton Regis Town Council

THAT WHICH WE CALL A STREET

Above-
The sign on Poynters Road, showing boundary between Houghton Regis and Dunstable, 2010 (SEG).

The way in which the streets in a town or village are named tells the story of its development and of the people who have been involved in its history. Houghton Regis has many examples of street names, which demonstrate its hidden past, and researching them has been a fascinating experience.

Occasionally, developers have strong views about the naming of their streets, but, in general, Houghton Regis Town Council plays a big role in determining how the streets on new developments are named. It is usual that the planning authority (Central Bedfordshire Council and, previously, South Bedfordshire District Council) ask the Town Council for suggestions. These are then taken through the Planning and Licensing Committee. Sometimes ideas are included for councillors' approval, based upon local knowledge, and the history of the area. At other times, suggestions are invited at the committee meeting itself. There are of course some names which never make it passed the Council Chamber doors, and others which are pure speculation! Once suggestions have been recorded, they are forwarded to the planning authority, who then in turn discuss the suggestions with the developers. Sometimes developers decide against the names suggested, and the roads may then be 'christened' something completely different altogether! However, if they have no real views on the street names, the decisions can then be taken at officer level by the planning authority.

In the past, some street naming decisions were made by Houghton Regis Parish Council (pre-1980), without the reasons being included in the minutes. It is unfortunate that, in some cases, the reasons for unusual names will never be known for sure. It is also worth noting that the Post Office is consulted by the planning authority, and many names for streets in Houghton Regis have been refused, owing to similarities to streets in Luton or Dunstable (the concern being that it could lead to post being delivered incorrectly). Examples of this have included titles such as 'Franklin', 'Repton' and 'Matthews', but, over the years, some street names have been duplicated between Luton and Dunstable, and most recently between Dunstable and Hockliffe. Others that have slipped through the net are 'Long Meadow' in Dunstable and 'Longmeadow' in Houghton Regis, and 'Rosedale' which has been used in both Houghton Regis and Sundon Park!

At the time of writing this book, most of the building taking place in Dunstable, and Houghton Regis, were estates rather than terraces or individual blocks of flats. With this in mind, Central Bedfordshire Council requested that these new estates be given themes running through them. One suggested reason for themes, is that it aides the emergency services!

It is important nevertheless that officers, councillors and developers consider the people who will one day be living in the properties. Some names sound great on paper and fit in with the surrounding streets, but the old saying about, 'a rose by any other name', certainly applies!

Left-
Lake View street sign Sept 2012 (SEG).

HOUGHTON HALL

Above-
Houghton Hall, The Green, taken in September 2009 (SEG).

The Houghton Hall area is located in the centre of Houghton Regis and takes its title from the magnificent building of the same name. Houghton Hall was built for Dame Alice Millard in 1700, and is located behind seven acres of public open space (The Village Green), which was transferred to the Town Council in 1954. Houghton Hall is no longer a private residence, and is currently the offices of Chamberlain Holdings.

The Houghton Hall area, is defined in electoral terms, as beginning at the border of Dunstable and Houghton Regis, outside All Saints Academy on Houghton Road. It also incorporates the hamlets of Sewell, Bidwell and Thorn, up to Tithe Farm Road, continuing from number 88 Houghton Road to Poynters Road and the border with Dunstable and Luton to the west of the town. This is the largest electoral division (referred to as a Ward) in Houghton Regis, and at the time of writing, included some 2,000 properties. The Houghton Hall Ward features most of the town's original buildings, some of which can be traced back to the 18th century. These buildings include The Chequers and The Crown Public Houses, Vane Cottage, Houghton Hall and the Red House. The most notable building in addition to Houghton Hall, is All Saints Parish Church, which is known to date from the 13th/14th century.

The central section of the Ward is one of over 8,000 Conservation Areas, which have been set up in England, since 1967. This means that the buildings are of special architectural or historic interest; this status is important in preserving the character of the area. The Conservation Area also takes in Woodlands Avenue, which was a post war housing development.

It is unfortunate that Houghton Regis has been subject to some boundary changes, with much land being taken away from the 'Parish' of Houghton Regis. The area today, known as High Street North, was formerly part of Upper Houghton, and was transferred to the Borough of Dunstable in 1907, against the wishes of the Houghton Regis residents, as shown in the Poll below. Further changes were made in April 1933, when a few local streets underwent a name change, during the expansion of the borough of Dunstable. One of these was Poynters Road, which was known as Park Road South, whilst Park Road North, which remained in Houghton Regis, retained its original name.

The boundary lines continued to change into the 1950s ,when the Brewers Hill Estate in Dunstable was built. The estate was originally incorporated into Houghton Regis, but was lost to Dunstable at this time. The Parish of Houghton Regis was not happy about this, and put up a strong case in their defence (1953), including what would be the resultant scandalous increase in rates! The last changes to Houghton's formation was in the 1980s, when the estates surrounding Frenchs Avenue were transferred to Dunstable.

Houghton Regis has continued to grow; with the Houghton Hall Ward seeing new developments in the 1980s, 1990s, 2000s and beyond. This has compensated for the areas lost in the past, and there are many more changes on the horizon, which will see further expansion in the near future, This development will help to secure Houghton Regis' future as an independent town.

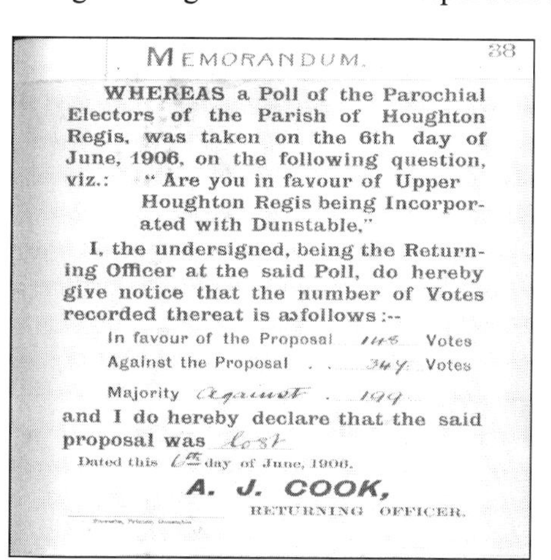

MEMORANDUM. 38

WHEREAS a Poll of the Parochial Electors of the Parish of Houghton Regis, was taken on the 6th day of June, 1906, on the following question, viz.: "Are you in favour of Upper Houghton Regis being Incorporated with Dunstable."

I, the undersigned, being the Returning Officer at the said Poll, do hereby give notice that the number of Votes recorded thereat is as follows :--

In favour of the Proposal 148 Votes

Against the Proposal . . 347 Votes

Majority against . 199

and I do hereby declare that the said proposal was lost

Dated this 6th day of June, 1906.

A. J. COOK,

RETURNING OFFICER.

Left -
A page from the Parish Council Minute Book showing the results of the Parochial Poll on 6th June 1906, regarding the loss of the area known as Upper Houghton to Dunstable. Reproduced by kind permission of Houghton Regis Town Council.

ALABASTER AVENUE

Left-
The land off Houghton Road being cleared in preparation for the 'Tilia Park housing development. April 2011 (SEG).

Alabaster Avenue is located on the 'Tilia Park' development (off Houghton Road), built at the edge of the quarry by Bovis Homes. The quarry was mined by Blue Circle Industries (formerly the Associated Portland Cement Manufacturers Ltd) from 1926 until 1971. There was also a Plant directly opposite the quarry, where the Townsend Industrial Estate now stands.

The Town Council originally submitted two sets of names for this new housing development; the first being names of birds, and, specifically, those which had been spotted in this area (e.g. Kingfisher's, Yellow Hammers, Cuckoos and Blackbirds). This was the preferred option of the Town Councillors, but it was felt by Development Control at Central Bedfordshire Council that this theme had been used extensively in many new developments. The second set of names was derived from connections from chalk and quarries.

Left-
An early advertisement promoting the housing development, March 2011 (SEG).
Right-
Alabaster Avenue March 2015 (SEG).

ARNALD WAY

There was an artist by the name of George Arnald who painted topical scenes of Bedfordshire, including Houghton Regis, and he lived from 1763 to 1841. It is known that George's father Thomas worked on the Brandreth Estate (Houghton Hall) and George was the same age as Henry Brandreth's son (also called Henry). It was thought that George was buried in All Saints Churchyard, but research through genealogy websites has shown that he died in the Pentonville area of London, and is presumably buried there. George Arnald's parents however are believed to be buried in the churchyard.

The street is located on the 'Priory Meadows' development, (although it was documented that 'Priory Meadows' is an area to the west of the Priory Church in Dunstable. Suggestions for other street names on the development were Corn Harvest Way and Quarry End.

With kind thanks to James Carroll for additional information about the Arnald family.

Left and above-
First houses on Arnald Way
during the mid 1990s.
Photos reproduced by kind
permission of Houghton
Regis Town Council.

BALMORAL ROAD

Left-
First houses on Balmoral Road under construction in October 2009 (SEG).

Balmoral Road is part of 'The Parc' development, which was started in 2009. As the streets were an extension of an existing area (built on land off Sandringham Drive), it was suggested that the names be continued along the same royal theme. The adopted names were suggested by Aldwyck Housing, Houghton Regis Town Council and Central Bedfordshire Council; names which didn't make the final list were Monarch's Way, Kew Gardens and Elizabeth Court.

BANKSIDE PLACE

Bankside Place is built on the site of Bankside Poultry Farm, which was run by Bernard Green. His mother Dorothy Green owned an arable farm, on which Roslyn Way is now situated.

BARLEYFIELD WAY

It is likely that this is a literal term, relating to the fields that were located where the houses were built. The name was suggested by Summit Homes, who built the properties. Incidentally, there is no number 13!

BEDFORD ROAD

BEDFORD COURT

Above-
A postcard from the early part of the last century showing All Saints Church, taken from Bedford Road.

Bedford Road is now a busy thoroughfare, which serves as the major route from the Town Centre to Bedford, via number of villages enroute; (hence its name). A quarter of a mile north of the Town Centre, at the Thorn Turn, is a link to the A5. Similarly there is link at the bottom end of the Bedford Road via the Town Centre along the High Street.

The picture at the top of the next page shows a shop at number 4 Bedford Road. On 24th September 1954, it was reported in the Luton News that Mr. Arthur George Auden, the father in law of Mr. Sidney Chaperlain, Headmaster of the Whitehead School, had suffered an accident on Bedford Road. Mr. Auden (aged 87, and of the School House, The Green) had gone to buy his usual packet of tobacco, when he fell in the road outside the shop. The shop assistant, Miss Margaret Adams, after witnessing the accident, ran out to Bedford Road to help Mr. Auden to his feet, sitting him in a chair for a while to recover. It was reported, however that the gentleman died in hospital from a type of Pneumonia, following a hip operation for a fractured Femur, incurred during the fall. The newspaper paper stated that "Sidney Chaperlain, Mr. Auden's son in law of The School House, The Green, Houghton Regis, said that Mr. Auden told him that, while crossing the road, he felt his leg give way and he just fell down, causing the fractured Femur".

Above-
A postcard from the early part of the last century showing the entrance to Bedford Road from the High Street.

Bedford Road, was also once home to The Cock Inn (owned by Messrs J.W Green Ltd) and there was a yard attached to this building. The pub/inn is mentioned in newspaper articles from the 1840s, right up to the 1920s, when it was seemingly mentioned no more.

In 1915, A Mr. Latham was reapplying for the license on the inn on behalf of tenant Mr. Alfred Ernest Bullock, when it seems as though the pub was under threat of closure. The newspaper stated that there were several licensed houses in the village, which belonged to one firm, and several to another. However Messrs J.W Green owned only this one, which was under threat. 'Every man was entitled to ask, and pay for a drink, and enjoy a glass of beer, and should surely be entitled, if he preferred Green's beer to have that" said Mr. Latham.

The Magistrates initially tried to blame the population for the proposed threat of closure, but Mr. Latham replied 'No I suggest that the Licensing Magistrate has something to do with it..!". Mr. Latham also compared the inn to 'One of those dear roadside inns that would have satisfied Dickens...thoroughly to the ground!"

It was proven that the pub was making enough trade to stay open, and an occasional license was granted in the meantime. The pub did remain open, but seemingly only for a few years.

Above-
The Old Red Lion photographed in July 2010 (SEG).

The other public house, which is still located on Bedford Road, (although technically in Bidwell), is The Old Red Lion.

Today, The Old Red Lion is a popular venue with a small private garden. There is a restaurant which serves a traditional pub menu and carvery meals.

A building appears on this site, on the Duke of Bedford's 1762 map, and there are stories about the pub/inn in the newspapers, during the late 19th century. It was reported as being the called 'Red Lion Inn' in the newspapers. As well as being used for the sale of beers and wines, pubs and inns were used in the way that public halls are utilised today. The pubs were used for inquests by magistrates, licensing reviews, and for public exhibition of houses, buildings and land for sale.

A former resident of the public house, is Trevor Turvey, who lived there with his family from 1933-1941. Trevor remembers the pub when there was an outside toilet, no bath (he says he understood the meaning of throwing the baby out with the bathwater!), and bats under the upstairs floorboards! In the summer there was no running water. The brewery at the Red Lion at this time was J.W Green's of Luton.

Trevor's mother and father were Violet and Jim Turvey and he lived at the Red Lion with sisters Millicent and Sylvia. During their days' at the Red Lion, it was frequented by a gentlemen called Will Carter, who was an ex WW1 veteran, without any known relatives. He lived in a Nissen hut in a field on a farm in Thorn Road. In the winter, Jim Turvey was known for his roaring fires in the tap room at the Old Red Lion, and Will would come in after opening time at 10, and buy half a pint of mild beer for two old pennies, and sit by the fire.

Often when Trevor returned home from school, (which was in Chiltern Road, Dunstable), Violet would give Mr. Carter some dinner. Trevor says that he would often go and chat to him, as there were few, if any, customers. Violet was an expert straw hat machinist, and Trevor would serve customers in the school holidays, when she had orders from Woolmer and Browning from Luton.

Trevor's older sister Millicent, and her husband Jim Fowler, later ran the Five Bells, in Houghton Regis, during the Second World War. The brewery required the pub to be open at 7, and Trevor would help, by opening up.

Trevor Turvey is the cousin of Bruce Turvey, of Turvey and Turvey Photographers. Bruce has told me that he remembers the days when Trevor lived at the Old Red Lion, 'as clear as yesterday', and they would often play at the Bluewaters (chalk pit), and Trevor says that living at Bidwell was heaven for small boys, with lots of trees to climb! Bluewaters was across the fields and they used to play in a disused chalk pit. Trevor often used to roam about with Harold Green of Dell Farm, but often used to sit with Buster Hines, who was an expert at plucking duck feathers, and preparing them for the London market. Harold also worked for Sonny Pratt, a local Butcher (almost opposite the church), who had a slaughter house at the back of his yard.

Following their time at The Red Lion, the family moved to The Green Man, at Chalk Hill, where Trevor lived until 1950, when he married at all Saints Church (with the reception at the National Schoolrooms). Mr. and Mrs. Turvey then lived at Drury Lane, Houghton Regis for twelve years. At some time during the 1950s, The Green Man was taken over by Millicent and Jim Fowler.

With thanks to Trevor and Bruce Turvey for their support which is greatly appreciated.

As well as houses and All Saints Parish (situated on the corner of street), Bedford used to be the location for allotments. The allotment land, was subject to Compulsory Purchase in the late 1950s. The original Vicarage House, adjacent to All Saints, was converted into Council Offices, for Luton and Rural District Council, in the 1960s and later demolished. This was to make way for Bedford

Court during the 1970s. The present day Vicarage House was built on a smaller plot next door; although it does boast a garden of about an acre in size.

BIDWELL HILL

BIDWELL CLOSE

Left-
An early postcard of Bedford Road, showing the houses on Bidwell Hill to the left. The steps beside the houses are still in situ and when this photo is enlarged, it is possible to see a little boy standing at the top of the stairs.

Bidwell Hill runs off Bedford Road. It leads to the hamlet of Bidwell, which points to the likely reason for this street name. Bidwell is recorded as 'Bidewell' on some historic documents. The older houses, on Bidwell Hill itself, were the first council houses built in the town, dating back to around 1919. In many documents, including the Parish Council Minutes and burial records, the addresses of these early properties are just recorded as 'Council Houses', with solely their street numbers.

The postcard picture, (overleaf), shows a house at the top of the steps on Bedford Road, but this was one of the four houses, on Bidwell Hill, which was demolished to build Bidwell Close. The road continued to be extended into the 1970s, and subsequently.

BLACKBURN ROAD

Left - The Rev. Leslie Blackburn taken at a Church Gift Day during November 1956. Photo reproduced by kind permission of John Buckledee/Dunstable Gazette.

Blackburn Road forms part of the industrial estate off Townsend Farm Road. There is no mention in the council's official records of the origin of the name, however there was a Reverend Leslie Blackburn, who was the Vicar of All Saints Parish Church, from 1952 to 1974, and it is virtually certain the street was named after him.

BRIDGEMAN DRIVE

Bridgeman Drive is located on the Painters Estate. There is no clear link to any artist, as is the case with other streets on the estate, but there is an art gallery in London called 'Bridgeman Art Library' (founded in 1972), which could possibly provide the answer to this street name.

BROOKFIELD AVENUE, CLOSE and WALK

Left-
An example of a 'Cornish' Type 1 PRC property of a similar design to those in the original Brookfield Estate. Taken Feb 2015 (SEG).

After both the World Wars had ended, there became a need to build houses for workers who were employed locally. Houses were built for these workers along Woodlands Avenue, Manor Park and the location, today, known as the Brookfield Estate. The houses on the Brookfield site were previously known as PRC properties, or Pre-fabricated Reinforced Concrete houses. These were eventually pulled down to make way for the modern estate during the late 1980s. This was undertaken by South Bedfordshire District Council, as part of the Urban Regeneration Scheme. The estate was mentioned in the council records as the Brookfield site, and from this, the names evolved. It would seem that the obvious reason for the name Brookfield is due to the small brook, which runs along Park Road North. The original suggestion for Brookfield Avenue was 'Brandreth Avenue' after the Brandreth Family, who once lived in Houghton Hall. Unfortunately the name was objected to by a resident of Brandreth Avenue, Dunstable, and the council then had to reconsider the name. On the original Brookfield Estate, there was a street called 'Chantry Court' (named after Chantry House, but now called 'Treów House) which contained three blocks of three storey flats.

Left-
A modern day picture of the houses on Brookfield Avenue. Taken Feb 2015 (SEG).

CEMETERY ROAD

Cemetery Road was named after the small cemetery located at the top of the street. For many years, the cemetery lay overgrown and undisturbed. From the mid 1980s the churchyard attached to All Saints Parish Church, was closed, as it had become too full to cater for any new burials. The old cemetery was then cleared, and put back into use from 1985. It is now well maintained, and used for all burials in Houghton Regis. Cemetery Road itself, was extensively extended, and this has been used for further housing development. The street was formerly known locally as 'Muddy Road' (a literal term) and 'Malmsey'.

It has been said that, following the renaming of the street as 'Cemetery Road', one resident, a Mr. Dickens, who lived in one of the older houses at the top of the street, refused to acknowledge the new street name!

The map commissioned by the Duke of Bedford in 1762 shows a large area in the locality of Cemetery Road, as being called 'Malmsey'. The definition of the word Malmsey, is a sweet red wine, but how it fits in with Houghton Regis is unclear. There are four houses on Cumberland Street, which go by the name of 'Malmsey Cottages'.

CHURCH END

There is no mention in the Council Minute Books about the naming of Church End, although it is likely to have a literal meaning. The only religious building, currently in this vicinity, is the Plymouth Brethren Church, off Bedford Road, although it is noted that this was built later than Church End. The land opposite was noted on the Duke of Bedford's Map as 'Church Hill', Church Field and Church Close, which may possibly provide the connection.

CLARENCE PLACE

Clarence Place is name of one of the block of flats on 'The Parc' development. This is named after Clarence House, which is the residence of the Prince of Wales and the Duchess of Cornwall.

CLARKES WAY

Above left-
Cllr S.C Clarke (taken in 1973 reproduced with kind permission of Central Bedfordshire Council
Above right-
Clarkes Way taken in April 2015 (SEG).

Clarkes Way was named in 1972 after Councillor S.C. Clarke MBE, JP (known as Sid Clarke), who was the Chairman of the Parish Council for many years, (including a 14 year run from 1963 to 1977). The original suggestion for this street was Clarke Road, before Clarkes Way was agreed upon. Cllr. Clarke was employed as a Toolmaker for Skefco Ball Bearing Co Luton, and originally lived on the High Street. He then moved to a house in Woodlands Avenue, and then a bungalow, on the same road, with a view across the Village Green. It has been said that Cllr. Clarke was very proud of The Green and indeed very protective! His bungalow was ideally situated to 'keep an eye on things'.

The photo of Cllr. Clarke was found in the Council Offices recently, and it is likely that it would have been on display, following the relocation of the council to its office in Peel Street in March 1976.

Cllr. Clarke's service to the council spanned from 1946 until he died in January 1981.

CONSTABLE CLOSE

In keeping with the rest of the Painters Estate, Constable Close was named after Artist John Constable.

COOPERS WAY

Hollywood Actor Gary Cooper (Frank James Cooper, born in Helena, Montana USA), was the grandson of Rebecca Freeman of the Freeman family, who worked the Mill on the High Street, for many generations in Houghton Regis. Rebecca Freeman married John Cooper, and emigrated, with their son Charles Henry Cooper (born in 1865), to America in 1883. During his life in England, it is believed that Charles spent much of his childhood at the White House, High Street, Houghton Regis, home of his Uncle, Josiah Freeman. While in America, Charles Cooper married Alice Augusta Louise Brazier (formerly of Gillingham, Kent).

Charles Cooper's parents, John and Rebecca (nee Freeman) once resided at Bull Farm, Watling Street, Hockliffe, Bedfordshire, before moving to Tingrith. The house is still standing, and has changed very little since those days.

Alice and Charles Cooper had two children; Arthur Leroy in 1895 and Frank James (Gary) in 1901. Charles became a Lawyer, Rancher and a Supreme Court Judge.

Gary was sent to England, along with his brother Arthur, in 1909, to be educated at the Dunstable Grammar School, which later became Ashton Middle School on High Street North. Both sons were baptised at All Saints Parish Church, in December of 1911. During their time in England, Gary, Arthur and Alice lived with first cousins, once removed on the Freeman side (Emily and Walter H Barton), at 157 High Street North, Dunstable. A blue heritage plaque has been erected by Dunstable Town Council to commemorate this.

On his return to America in August 1912, Gary continued his education at Johnson

Left-
Gary Cooper (far left) with his brother Arthur (far right).
Photo reproduced by kind permission of Maria Cooper Janis.

Left-
The Cooper residence in Hockliffe, Bedfordshire, (the house has changed very little. Since the picture was taken). Photo reproduced by kind permission of Maria Cooper Janis.
Below left-
Photograph of the plaque above 157 High Street North, Dunstable, 2015 (SEG).

Grammar school in Helena. A car accident at the age of 15 resulted in the damaging of his hip, and he was advised to recover by taking up horseback riding. It is reported that this advice may have created his trademark walking and slightly angled riding styles! In 1924 Charles and Alice moved to Los Angeles, and Gary followed later that year. It was in 1925 that he became a film extra and stunt rider, and changed his name from Frank James to Gary (after the place Gary, Indiana). In 1929, Gary Cooper became a major movie star with the release of his first movie with sound. The rest , as they say , is history!

Gary married actress Veronica Balfe (stage name Sandra Shaw), and they had one daughter Maria, who was born in 1937. Gary Cooper died in 1961 of Prostate Cancer, but Maria Cooper Janis told me that he did visit Dunstable one last time, whilst filming his final movie 'The Naked Edge' at Elstree Studios. He took a drive passed his old school, without stopping, but pointed out a tree to his daughter, where some 'fisticuffs' had broken out many years before!

I asked Maria what her father would have thought about having a street named after him, and she believes that he would have been very proud.

With thanks to Maria Cooper Janis for all the additional information, the family photographs and support, which is greatly appreciated.

COPPERFIELDS CLOSE

Copperfields was the development name chosen by Messrs Westbury Homes, for Copperfields Close, which was an extension to 'Area 5', (see map on page 59) in the early 1990s. The properties off Windsor Drive, on both sides of the road, were built on land that once belonged to Poynters Farm.

Left-
The logo from the sales brochure for 'Copperfields', 'A superb development of stunning 2 & 3 bedroom homes at Houghton Regis, Dunstable.' Reproduced with kind permission of Roger Marsh & Co.

CUMBERLAND STREET

CUMBERLAND COURT

Above-
A postcard from the early part of the century showing the High Street. The White Horse Public House is on the corner of Cumberland Street. Prior to redevelopment of the town, Cumberland Street was in two sections with Queen Street in the middle.

It is known that Mr. Richard Cumberland (died May 30th 1874, aged 87) was the Headmaster of Whiteheads Free School for 53 years. It is not known for sure where the street name originates, but it seems possible that there is a connection to Mr. Cumberland, owing to his high profile position in the town, and his long standing service. It is also not certain when Cumberland Street was built, although it is recorded in the 1881 census, and the style of building is typical of Victorian architecture.

Left-
The gravestone of Richard Cumberland in All Saints Churchyard September 2014 (SEG).

It is difficult to explain to modern day 'Houghtonians' about the layout of the original Cumberland Street, and there is often a lot of misunderstanding. This is because Cumberland Street was in two sections and the first section was accessed via the High Street. Queen Street ran cross the centre, followed by the second half of Cumberland Street (as it is now). The top half of Cumberland Street was lost during the redevelopment of the High Street, in the late 1960s, having been located where the Morrisons Supermarket now stands.

Left-
Cumberland Street taken in 2009 (SEG).

Cumberland Court is a recent addition to Cumberland Street and was chosen to provide continuity.

DOUGLAS CRESCENT

Above-
A Street Party in Douglas Crescent at the end of the Second World War. Photo reproduced with kind thanks to Mary Sidgwick (née Holt)

Douglas Crescent, built by Mead Estates Ltd, is situated on the border of Houghton Regis and Dunstable. The crescent shaped street comprises semis, terraces and detached properties.

William Mead (the founder of Mead Estates), was born in 1895, and he started the company in 1934, building houses in the Luton and Dunstable area. The land, on which Douglas Crescent now stands, was owned by the Beecroft Family, who once possessed the area on which the Beecroft Estate was built.

Brewers Hill Farm in Dunstable, was farmed for many generations by the Cook Family, and Miss Alice Mary Cook (born 1855) married Edward Robert Beecroft in

Above left-
Some of the workers hand digging foundations on some new properties.
Above right-
William Mead and his third wife Minnie.
Photographs reproduced by kind permission of Mead Estates Ltd.

1879. The Beecroft Family sold off the land in Dunstable to Dunstable Borough Council, during the 1930s, for the building of houses, after having built a few houses on the land themselves. The land, on which Douglas Crescent stands, was sold by Mr. and Mrs. Beecroft to Meads, also during the 1930s.

A planning application was submitted by Mead Estates to build a pair of semi detached houses in 1936, but house building stopped, in 1939, presumably owing to the outbreak of Second World War. It is known that during this time, the company focused on repairing bomb damaged houses in the London area. William and his first wife had three children, Audrey, Peter and Douglas, and the road is named after this youngest son.

In April 1948, the Parish Council was asked to suggest possible sites to Luton and Rural District Council, for the building of council houses (for a waiting list of local tenants). One of the areas suggested was the 'undeveloped land at Douglas Crescent'. This however was not utilised, and instead Manor Park was created. The house building by Meads, continued in 1951, with detached and semi detached houses erected. This also accounts for the difference in the style of houses.

THE LUTON NEWS, Thursday, August 6, 1953—3

HOUSES!!

A home built to your requirements

Our present bookings are for houses to be completed 30th January, 1954. We are now booking for houses to be completed February/May, 1954.

Houghton Regis

(Dunstable) DOUGLAS CRES., off Houghton Road

SEMI-DETACHED **£1,835** DETACHED **£1,985**

Including Land — Large Garden — Garage Space

THE BEST VALUE OBTAINABLE

Write or phone to let us know when convenient for you to inspect completed houses. We shall be pleased to give full information regarding deposit and monthly repayments of mortgage.

MEAD ESTATES *Ltd.*

Builders PRINCES ST., DUNSTABLE *Phone 115*

Above left-
Advert for the new houses on Douglas Crescent from August 1953. Advert reproduced by kind permission of the Luton News.

Above right-
84 Douglas Crescent with two of the first occupants, Lesley and Carol Underwood. Photo reproduced with kind thanks to David Underwood.

Left-
Friends from Douglas Crescent on their bikes. Gary Griffiths is pictured in the left and Clive Jones on the right, next to the Underwood family's pet Cat. Sadly the identity of the cyclist in the centre is unknown.
Mr. Underwood can be seen in the background of number 84 working on a boat that he made.
Photo reproduced with kind thanks to David Underwood.

Mead Estates was based in Princes Street, Dunstable until 2004, when it was relocated to Ridgmont, in Bedfordshire. The company continues to be managed by William's grandchildren, Geoffrey, Richard and Janet.

Many friends on the 'Up Above The Streets and Houses', and 'Houghton Regis Back In The Day' Facebook pages, have provided information about a shop, which was sited on the corner of Douglas Crescent and Houghton Road. The shop, (called Mansers), was on the 'Dunstable side' of Douglas Crescent and stocked Lucozade, Tizer, threepenny ice lollies and 'everything from food to toys' amongst the product range.

With kind thanks to Susan Slough for additional information about the Beecroft and Cook Family.

DOUGLAS PLACE

Douglas Place is a recent addition, comprising a few properties on Douglas Crescent, being so named for continuity.

DUNSTABLE ROAD

It is likely that Dunstable Road was given its name because of its proximity to the border of Dunstable and Dog Kennel Walk, (the footpath which runs between Houghton Regis and Dunstable). There was also a field name of 'Dunstable Path Furlong' in this approximate location.

Left-
Dog Kennel
Down, pictured in
2010 (SEG).

EAST END

Above-
An early postcard showing the 'Chequers Public House' along East End.

The Duke of Bedford's 1762 map shows the area to the east of the town as being 'East Hill', and it seems logical that East End is just a literal term for the eastern part of the town. The picture above shows The Chequers during the early part of the last century, and it was certainly trading as far back as 1855, when the brewery was noted as being 'Ashdown Bros'. The building is located within the Conservation Area, but is surprisingly, not classed as a listed building.

Research, through old newspapers, has shown some very interesting stories; noteworthy, was the fact that the Licensee, Mr. William Clark, was fined for opening his house to sell beer between 3pm and 5pm on a Sunday in 1856. Did he learn his lesson? He was fined again in 1857, but this time for opening his house to sell beer before 12.30pm on a Sunday!

The Licensed Victualler (Landlady) in 1881 was a Mrs. Ann Hill, who was born in Cheddington, Buckinghamshire in about 1813. Ann's story is a strange and sad one. She married husband George Hill at the Union Workhouse in Luton, in 1862, and is listed on the 1871 census of Houghton Regis at The Red Lion, High Street, (possibly a clerical error) with her daughter (Clara Edwins, born 1854 also in Cheddington).

Above-
The same view of 'The Chequers' taken in 2009 (SEG).

George Hill became the Licensee of The Chequers in 1862, after the license was transferred from a David White. However George was not listed in the town at all on any of the census returns from 1861 to 1881, and Ann was granted a Protection Order in 1878, after George had abandoned her, and she hadn't seen him for nine years. Ann was shown on the 1881 census of Houghton Regis as a 'Widower', with son in law Edwin Sharp, a Coach Painter, and daughter Clara, a Straw Machinist, at the same address.

However, on 12th November 1883, Ann suffered a terribly shocking death, after she went into a fit, whilst carrying out household duties, and fell into the fire. Her groans attracted the attentions of the Postmistress who was delivering letters at the time. She was found frightfully burnt but conscious, although the Postmistress was not strong enough to remove her from her position. There was a delay in obtaining some help to move Ann, and a man's assistance was asked for, but he refused, on account of the fact that he had to go to work! Eventually, she was removed from the fire. Ann died that same night.

Seven years later in January 1891, the pub fell victim to a disastrous fire, which destroyed the building and two adjoining thatched cottages. Although well equipped, the Fire Brigade were unable to put the fire out, owing to the fact that the water supply was frozen. Nothing could be done to save the inn. The fire took the life of a local labourer by the name of William Robinson, who was killed by falling from a chimney stack, and several other men were injured. The cause of the fire has not been recorded.

Another historic pub which is located in East End, is The Crown Public House, which is also shown on the Duke of Bedford's 1762 map.

The pub is very old, and it has been said that part of the pub has been dated back as far as the 1600s. What is known for sure, is that in 1904, the pub was faced with closure and the Landlady (Mrs. Ann Allen) was faced with having to make some repairs, in order to keep the house open.

Over the past one hundred years, the Landlord's of the pub (who are remembered with affection) have included Mr. Meacham, Ted Ledo, Alan Johns and his wife Freda.

Above-
Mrs. Freda Johns, who was Landlady of The Crown from the 1960s to the 1980s. Alan Johns was the Landlord. Photo Reproduced with kind permission of Mrs. P Cameron.

Above-
The inside of the back bar. Alan Johns liked to decorate with lots of brass items. Photo reproduced with kind permission of Mrs. P Cameron.

Left-
The Crown pictured in 2011, dressed up for the Royal Wedding (SEG).

EVANS CLOSE

Above-
An event organised by Vauxhall Motors in September 1998. Edryd Evans is on the right hand side of the picture on the second row. With thanks to Mrs. M Tommey. Photo reproduced by kind permission of Vauxhall Motors.

Mr. William (Edryd) Evans, was Clerk to Houghton Regis Parish and Town Council for 37 Years between 1953 and 1990. Evans Close was named in 1992, in honour of Mr. Evans' service to the community.

The above picture was taken at the Vauxhall Parts and Accessories Depot in Boscombe Road, Dunstable, and includes dignitaries such as the Chairman of South Bedfordshire District Council, Councillor Peter Rawcliffe, the Chairman of Bedfordshire County Council (and also the Town Mayor of Houghton Regis during this time), Councillor John Kinchella, the Mayor of Dunstable, Councillor Mrs. Brenda Boatwright, the Deputy Mayor of Houghton Regis, Councillor Dave Barratt, and Richard Walden, Town Clerk to Dunstable Town Council. John Costin from Vauxhall Motors is pictured at the right of the photograph next to Councillor Mrs. Boatwright, and Edryd Evans is standing immediately behind, on the second row.

FARRIERS WAY

Left-
View of The Quarry taken from Farriers Way taken in 2011 (SEG).
Below-
Photos from The Discovery Channel film shoot at The Quarry.
Photos reproduced by kind permission from The Wildlife Trust.

Farriers Way is a street located on the 'Priory Meadows' development, which is situated at the former quarry/chalk pit. Houghton Regis Town Council's preferred name for Farriers Way was 'Matthews Way' after C.L Matthews, who led the excavation of Puddlehill during the 1960s. However South Bedfordshire District Council was unable to accept this name, owing to its similarity to 'Matthew Street' Dunstable, which shares the same postal sorting office. Therefore it was agreed that the street would be called 'Farriers Way' as a companion to Millers Way.

It is known that the film 'Man In the Moon', starring Kenneth Moore, was filmed in the chalk pit in 1960, as was an Episode of Dr Who, starring Patrick Troughton, where the Tardis can be seen materialising over The Quarry! More recently the area has been looked after by The Wildlife Trust, and the Chalk Pit was used for location filming in 2011, by The Discovery Channel masquerading as a 'Tibetan Village'.

FIELDSTONE

Fieldstone is a recent addition to the town on the 'Tilia Park' Estate, and was still under construction at the time of writing. It carries on the quarrying theme, which is featured throughout the estate. The quarry can be viewed from the end of this road.

FREEMANS CLOSE

Above left-
Josiah Freeman was the last Miller to work the mill on the High Street. Photo courtesy of the Dunstable Gazette, John Buckledee /The Pat Lovering Collection.
Above right-
Freemans Close taken February 2015 (SEG).

It is widely known, that Houghton Regis used to be home to a Corn Mill, which was situated at the top of 'Mill Road', where the Priory Meadows development is now located. What isn't so well known, is that there was a second operational mill on the corner of, what is now Whitehouse Close.

The mill on the High Street was worked for generations by the Freeman Family. Josiah Freeman (born 1837), the Great Uncle of Hollywood Actor, Gary Cooper), was the last Miller to work in the High Street.

FROGMORE ROAD

Left-
Frogmore Road under construction October 2009 (SEG).

The Frogmore Estate (including Frogmore House) is located within the grounds of the Home Park, adjoining Windsor Castle in Berkshire. It is believed that the name 'Frogmore' comes from the large number of frogs, which have always lived in that area, owing to the localised topography! Frogmore Road, Houghton Regis is on 'The Parc' Estate which runs off Sandringham Drive. The name was chosen to continue the royal theme of existing streets.

GAINSBOROUGH DRIVE

Gainsborough Drive on the Painters Estate, gets its name from the Artist Thomas Gainsborough (1727-1788). Gainsborough's most notable works were 'The Blue Boy' and 'Mr. and Mrs. Andrews'.

GILPIN CLOSE

Rev. William Gilpin (1724-1804) was an English Artist, Clergyman, Schoolmaster and Author. The decision to name the estate was taken by the builders, who wanted themes running through the street names.

HALLEYS WAY

Above-
Halleys Way April 2015 (SEG).

Halleys Way was built by MacLean Homes in 1986, and is named after 'Halley's Comet', which made a famous appearance that year. The Comet is named after Sir Edmond Halley (1656-1742), the English Astronomer who calculated the comet's orbit in 1705.

Halley's Comet is seen every 75-76 years, and as it was last seen in 1986, it will therefore, next be seen in 2061-2062.

HAMPTON PLACE

Hampton Place is the name of one of the blocks of flats on 'The Parc' development.

Hampton Place is named after Hampton Court Palace, which dates back to at least the mid 15th century, when it was a Medieval Manor.

HARRINGTON HEIGHTS

A young man called Bob Harrington, worked in the Drawing Office of the builders M.J Shanley during the 1970s. Bob was involved with the Bidwell Hill Development when he worked for the company, and he was the first employee to have a street named after him!

HIGH STREET

Above-
Photograph taken from the Church Tower showing houses on the High Street prior to the redevelopment in the 1960s. Photograph reproduced with kind permission of the Dunstable Gazette/John Buckledee.

The High Street in Houghton Regis dates back to beyond the 1870s, when it was the centre of business and trade. The street was packed with shops, pubs, small family run businesses and houses. Before this, there was a main street in the town, but it is possible that it went by the name of Town Street as opposed to High Street, as evidenced by the 1841 census.

The pubs or inns on the High Street included the Five Bells, The White Horse, The Unicorn and The Kings Arms (the later being built on land belonging to the Manor of Houghton Regis).

The original Kings Arms Pub, which is featured in the postcard below, is on the site of the present pub, which goes by the same name. The present pub was built in 1936 and it is said that this was due to a chimney fire on the original building. A local resident, Mrs. Pamela Cameron, remembers the 'new' Kings Arms being built as she used to roller skate on the corner, where the pub now stands!

During the early part of the 20th century, many pubs were inspected at the time of license transfers and renewals, and this lead to some being pulled down and rebuilt, owing to their poor state. The Five Bells was one such pub, which was forced to improve, although its demise came eventually owing to the redevelopment of the High Street.

Above -
A postcard from the early part of the last century showing the original Kings Arms Public House on the corner of the High Street and Bedford Road.

The Five Bells was situated on the High Street, Houghton Regis, in the approximate location of where the junction of Cemetery Road and the High Street meet today. In 1904, it was claimed (when faced with closure), that the pub dated back to the 1600s.

Above -
The Five Bells, High Street, Houghton Regis featured on a postcard in 1914.

The above postcard was sent on 7th December 1914 from a gentleman in Houghton Regis, to a lady in North Lambeth, London. It reads" Dear Nellie. Arrived safely in the early hours of the morning in the pouring rain, and am now feeling a bit tired. Mud down here is worse than ever. This is a photo of the High Street but you cannot see my place as its out of the picture. Trusting you are quite well, with love Charlie".

Unfortunately many of the original High Street buildings were pulled down during the re-development of Houghton Regis in the 1950s and 1960s. Compulsory Purchase Orders were placed on properties in the top section of Cumberland Street, houses on King Street and the whole of Albert Road. During the latter part of the 1960s, according to local people, the houses were totally habitable some having been in families for many years. It was during the redevelopment of the area that The Five Bells was pulled down. Other places which have disappeared over time include 'Wrights Yard' and 'Folly's Yard', (which were believed to be off the High Street).

The Five Bells was managed by many Landlord's, which included Mr. and Mrs. Fowler, Mr. and Mrs. Thorpe, and Mr. and Mrs. Walmsley. At one time, The Five Bells used to operate a Christmas savings club, where two shillings a week were deposited throughout the year. The funds were then withdrawn at the end of the year, ready for the seasonal expenses. During the time that Mr. and Mrs. Thorpe were in charge, there were coach trips organised (more often than not) to Southend.

Above left-
A coach trip organised by The Five Bells during the early 1950s. Mrs. Thorpe is standing, and Mrs. Kitney is at the front, with Vera Swales sitting at the rear of the picture.
Photo reproduced by kind thanks to Mrs. P Cameron.

Above right-
The ladies pictured with Eric Puddefoot (Driver of the Costins Coach).
Photo reproduced by kind thanks to Mrs. P Cameron.

Left-
The gentlemen on one of The Five Bells Coach Trip.
Photo reproduced by kind permission of Mrs. Jean Cheshire.

Some of the businesses, which were once found on the High Street, included Tansley's Fish and Chip Shop, Jasper Perry's shop, Pratt's the Butchers and Higgs the Cobblers. The High Street also included The Workhouses, Tithe Farmhouse and the Fire Station. Bedford Square Shopping Centre was opened in 1966 and this has been the main shopping area in the town ever since.

Above-
Photograph of the High Street taken from the Church Tower showing a similar perspective to the previous picture, on page 39. Whitehouse Close is to the right of the picture. Reproduced by kind permission of David Hill (2003).

The Co-op store in the picture above, was built during the early 1980s, with the social club above, completed in 1986. The most recent changes to the High Street have taken place since the disastrous fire of June 2006, in which the Co-op store including the Houghton Regis Centre (Social Club) were destroyed. The fire was started deliberately on a warm summer evening, and the blaze spread quickly from dry vegetation at the side of the building to the Social Club above. Over 100 fire crew were in attendance to extinguish the fire, which was reported as being one of the worst in Bedfordshire for some time. The large supermarket was destroyed completely and had to be demolished for safety reasons.

The Co-op store was able to trade again from a corner building, for about seven years, before finally closing its doors in June 2014. The building was demolished in March 2015, and, at the time of writing, the site was under consultation for redevelopment.

Left-
The Co-op after the blaze in which the shop and Social Club were destroyed. Taken in June 2006 (SEG).

A new Morrisons Supermarket was opened further down the High Street in November 2012. The store was built on the former 'AA Insulations' site (which had stood vacant for many years), and, where the industrial units, which backed on to Queen Street were sited. The site had previously been earmarked, in the Town Centre Masterplan of 2007, for mixed use residential and retail units, but there had been little interest in the site for residential purposes, owing to the economic situation at this time. The site was eventually acquired for Morrisons, who invested £12 million in the project, which included changes to the High Street layout, with the installation of roundabout, to assist the traffic flow through the town. The company traded as a mini supermarket from the former Netto building (on corner of High Street and Cemetery Road), for about two years, whilst the store was being built.

Left-
The Netto store on corner of the High Street and Cemetery Road taken in the 1990s. Photograph reproduced by kind permission of Houghton Regis Town Council.

HOLYROOD DRIVE

Left-
Holyrood Drive taken in March 2015 (SEG).

Holyrood Drive (part of The Parc development) was built in 2009. The street was named after the Palace of Holyrood House in Edinburgh. The Queen is resident at Holyrood House during Holyrood week, which takes place at the end of June/early July. The street name continues the 'royal' theme which runs through the estate.

HOUGHTON ROAD

Left-
The stone indicating the Dunstable Borough Border with Houghton Regis as established in 1933 (SEG).

Houghton Road is self evident, in that the street leads to Houghton Regis. However Houghton Road used to be known as 'Mixt Way', which comes from 'Mixt Way Furlong' as shown on the Duke of Bedford's 1762 map. The name 'Mixt' is said to come from waste that was dumped on the land! The road was divided up between Dunstable and Houghton Regis, during boundary changes. The stone outside All Saints Academy, on Houghton Road, denotes the border between the two towns, which dates back to 1933.

KEATON CLOSE

Keaton Close started life as 'Repton Close', a name suggested by the developer. Unfortunately the Post Office objected to the name, owing to the fact that there was already a 'Repton Close' in Bramingham, Luton. The Post Office was concerned that using the name twice might cause confusion, and an alternative name for the street was sought. The next suggested name was 'Steer Close' but this was subsequently dropped, and the Town Council eventually suggested Keaton Close.

KENSINGTON CLOSE

Kensington Close is named after Kensington Palace continuing the royal theme of the streets.

KING STREET

Left-
The last industrial unit to be demolished on corner of High Street and Cemetery Road in March 2012 (SEG).
The units once stretched across to King Street with AA Insulations being located in front of the buildings facing on to the High Street. The units were demolished to make way for the Morrisons store.

King Street (off the High Street) is one of the original roads in Houghton Regis, which is still standing today, although not in its original format. The road once featured Victorian styled terraced housing on both sides, but was subject to compulsory purchase orders during the late 1960s. The houses were demolished and 'Bierrum House' was built on one corner adjoining the High Street (as an Air Call Doctor's Surgery) and industrial units were built on the opposite corner and on both sides of the road. Walkley Road was built at the end of King Street during the 1940s.

KINGSLAND CLOSE

Kingsland Close (1988) was named after the Kingsland Community College, (which later closed in August 1999).

LAKE VIEW

Left-
First houses on Lake View taken August 2011 (SEG).

Lake View forms the main road on the 'Tilia Park' Estate, and was literally named. The author admits responsibility for this street name!

LIMESTONE GROVE

Limestone Grove came from the original suggestions from the Town Council and is a reference to the quarrying which took place on the site.

LONGBROOKE

Owing to its location, this is an obvious choice of name, as the road is 'along by the brook', that runs along Park Road North. It is quoted in the Council Minutes in 1986 as land south of 'Houghton Brooke', and the street name was originally suggested as being 'Long Brook'. The street was built by Tarmac Homes Ltd.

LOWRY DRIVE

Left-
St Thomas' Meeting House on Lowry Drive 2006. Photo reproduced by kind permission of Houghton Regis Town Council.

Lowry Drive was named after L.S Lowry, the painter who was famous for his matchstick drawings and scenes of Manchester. The name continues the theme of artists on the 'Painters Estate'.

The picture above shows St Thomas' Meeting House, which was opened in 1988, being designed as an extension to All Saints Church, to accommodate more members, after the Parkside Estate was completed. Prior to the building if this new Church, the members used to meet at number 7 Enfield Close', the home of Rev. Christopher Samuels.

MANOR PARK

MANOR CLOSE

The area, where Manor Park and Manor Close are sited, used to belong to Mr. Sandford, who owned the bakery on Queen Street. The area was taken under a Compulsory Purchase Order, and it was rumoured that some locals believed that the name should be called 'Sandford's' Folly'.

Houghton Hall was once a large Manor House with an extensive amount of land. There was also Manor Farm, which was located where part of Clarkes Way is today. It is possible that Manor Park has been thus named, because of the fact that the land backs on to this area.

MAYER WAY

Left-
Car dealership on Mayer Way, taken July 2010 SEG).

Terry Mayer was the owner of the 10.92 acre site, which was developed in 1997. The site had previously been home to the Associated Portland Cement Works (Blue Circle Industries), but had fallen into a state of disrepair after the site closed. Terry Mayer was the owner of the Bradhill Trading Company, which owned the site for a short time, before outline planning permission was granted for the Industrial Estate.

The Town Council suggested the name 'The Regis Industrial Park, Regis Way' but the name Mayer Way was suggested by the developers, Palisander Properties.

Left-
Mayer Way showing the Arc Car wash and Houghton Road prior to the Tilia Park housing development in July 2010 (SEG).

MILL ROAD

Left-
The Mill at the top of Mill Road. Reproduced by kind permission of the Dunstable Gazette/John Buckledee.

Mill Road was named after the Mill, which was once located at the top of this road *(see Millers way, Freemans Close)*. The original houses on Mill Road, and the houses on Townsend Terrace, were built by Blue Circle Industries during the late 1920s, essentially as homes for its workers.

MILLERS WAY

Left-
The remains of the Corn Mill (taken in March 1976) which is located at the top end of what is now Millers Way. Photograph reproduced by kind permission of Tom Burnham.

Millers way is located next to Mill Road, from where the name originates.

MILTON WAY

Abovc-
Poynters Farm. Photo reproduced by kind thanks to Jane Lousada (née Blow).

As with Tennyson Avenue, Milton Way was named, following a suggestion from South Bedfordshire District Council, that the new streets, built in this development, should have a theme running through them. These roads were all named with a literary connection in mind. Milton Way was named after John Milton, who lived from 1608-1674 being best known for his work 'Paradise Lost' .

The land that Halley's Way, Milton Way and Tennyson Avenue were built on, was once Poynters Farm.

The farm was once owned by A.J Cook, who passed away in 1910. Following this, the farm was taken over by Young Jen Blow (father of Ernest Garratt Blow, and grandfather of Leonard Jack Blow (*see Tithe Farm and Easthill Farm).* The picture above shows the front of the house.

One of the workers at Poynters Farm, was Shepherd (Sonny) Ward, who was the father of Percy Ward, who owned the Queen Street Bakery.

Above-
Young Jen
Blow at
Codicote Bury
in Welwyn,
Hertfordshire,
before his
arrival at
Poynters Farm.
Left-
Shepherd Ward
at Poynters
Farm in 1928.
Photos
reproduced with
kind thanks to
Jane Lousada
(née Blow).

MOORE CRESCENT

Above-
The official opening of the Moore Crescent Sports Pavilion in May 2010. Photo reproduced by kind permission of Houghton Regis Town Council.

For many years the Renault Sports Ground occupied the site, now known as Moore Crescent. There was also a clubhouse for 'Houghton Town Sports and Social Club' (HTSCC) which shared the grounds, but it was known locally as the 'Renault Club'.

Moore Crescent was named in 1999, after a steward of the club, who was called 'Tony Moore'. He served the club for approx. 20 years until 1993. Mr. Moore died in the late 1990s and his family, who still remain local, were asked for permission to name the street in his memory.

A permanent home for the Houghton Regis Bowls Club was built adjacent to the Bowls Green in Moore Crescent. The Moore Crescent Sports Pavilion was opened by Town Mayor, Councillor Robin Hines, in May 2010.

Above-
The Champagne flows at the opening of the Pavilion with refreshments provided by Houghton Regis Bowls Club (left Tina Wills and right, Pauline Heather), May 2010.
Below-
A game of Bowls in Progress! May 2010. Photographs reproduced by kind permission of Houghton Regis Town Council.

NASH CLOSE

Nash Close on the 'Painters Estate' could have been named after Paul Nash 1889-1946, who was a surrealist painter, war artist, writer and photographer or John Nash 1893-1977, who was a British landscape painter.

NORTHVIEW ROAD

Northview Road, off Houghton Road, is likely to be a literal name.

ORCHARD CLOSE

The bungalows in Orchard Close were constructed during 1970. The names Greenway/Green Close, Meadow Close and Sycamore Close were all suggested, but the Parish Council agreed that the name Orchard Close be submitted. The area used to be home to a bungalow belonging to Mrs. Welford (called Vermont) and a smallholding, which contained two orchards.

Above-
The area which is now Orchard Close and Cemetery Road, as seen from one of the towers of the Portland Cement works around 1930. Photo reproduced with kind permission of Richard Goosey.

Mrs. Pamela Cameron (née Palmer) lived with Mrs. Welford. her grandmother, after her parents passed away, when she was a baby. Mrs. Welford grew many different varieties of apple in the orchards, which included Blenheim, Russets and Beauty of Bath. The Russets though, along with Greengages and some pears were never sold, and were kept to be eaten at home!

Mrs. Welford used to take in evacuees during the Second World War and there were soldier's billeted at her home. It is thought that as many as 82 people passed through the bungalow at this time. Some only stayed for a couple of days, where as one little girl stayed all through the war, and for a year afterwards. Mrs. Welford also took in a local girl called Joan, after her mother (who was a friend) passed away.

Following Mrs. Welford's death, the bungalow and land was sold during 1965/1966, although initially one of the local authorities had opposed the sale for house building, owing to the additional traffic on the High Street! In place of Vermont and the smallholding, 13 bungalows were built. Originally the builders had hoped to try to retain a tree from the orchards in each garden.

With thanks to Mrs. Cameron for additional information, support and photographs.

Above-
Mr. Charlie James and Joan, pictured in the garden of 'Vermont' on the 'Malmsey Estate' during August 1961. Photo reproduced by kind permission of Mrs. P Cameron.

Above-
Miss Pamela Palmer, aged 16 with her dog Rolo.
Photo reproduced by kind permission of Mrs. P Cameron.

PARK ROAD NORTH

Left-
The Funeral of Second Lt. Bertlin in July 1915 taken by Charles Smy. This postcard has been reproduced by kind permission of Mr. Dudley Smy.

Park Road North is one of the entry roads into Houghton Regis, and its origin is most likely derived from Houghton Hall Park. Poynters Road, which leads into Luton and Dunstable, was originally called 'Park Road South', until the boundary lines were redrawn in 1933. The oldest house, still standing on Park Road North is' Vane Cottage', which is a Grade II listed property.

In July 1915, a huge Military funeral took place in the village of Houghton Regis for a Soldier, who was tragically killed on Park Road North, whilst on active service. Second Lieutenant Hugh Antony Bertlin (born 1891 in the Republic of Argentina to English parents), was stationed on the Village Green, whilst serving with the Royal Engineers. He was driving a motorcycle by The Chequers Inn (pub), after setting off from Houghton Regis towards Luton, when he collided with a car being driven in the opposite direction. The driver of the Sunbeam (Frederick Percival Jones from Dunstable) had tried to avoid the collision, by running his car into a fence, but the motorcycle hit the vehicle, throwing the driver and his passenger into the road.

Lt. Bertlin was unconscious and was taken by car to the gates of Houghton Hall, where he was treated by the Royal Army Medical Corps. However, as he had suffered head injuries, and remained comatose, Second Lieutenant Bertlin was taken by Ambulance to Wardown Park Military Hospital, in Luton, where he died two days later (12th July 1915), without regaining consciousness. He had been stationed in Houghton Regis for only ten days before the accident occurred.

Two weeks later, an inquest was held into the accident. It heard much conflicting evidence, including whether the car had sounded its horn, was the motorcycle being driven on the wrong side of the road, and variations about the speed at which the car was travelling. It was also noted that the accident occurred at a dangerous corner with a 9ft hedge obstructing visibility, and the inquest recommended that a warning post sign be erected there. The verdict was recorded as 'Accidental Death'. Lt. Bertlin is buried in the churchyard at All Saints Parish Church.

Above-
The Funeral of Second Lt. Bertlin in July 1915 taken by Charles Smy. This postcard has been reproduced by kind permission of Mr. Dudley Smy.**The above story of Lt. Bertlin written by the author (as amended), was originally published in the Dunstable Gazette in 2010**.

PARKSIDE CLOSE

Although situated in the Houghton Hall Ward, Parkside Close was built during the 1980s and is situated off Parkside Drive. The name was chosen for continuity purposes.

PLAITERS WAY

'Plaiter' was the surname of one of the staff who was connected with M.J Shanley, the builders. During this time, many of the staff were immortalised by having streets named after them!

PORTLAND CLOSE

Left-
A postcard, which was posted in 1940 showing the Cement Works on Townsend Road. The wall is still visible today.

Portland Close is located on the Townsend Farm Industrial Estate and the name comes from the 'Associated Portland Cement Manufacturers'. The Cement Works, which later went under the name 'Blue Circle Industries', was located on the west side of the town, where the industrial estate now stands.

PORTLAND RIDE

There were three suggestions put forward to South Bedfordshire District Council, for the street now known as 'Portland Ride'. Those suggestions were New Park Ride, Pointers Walk/Pointers Croft and Portland Ride. The name Portland Ride was finally selected, and it seems very likely that the choice is related to the 'Associated Portland Cement Manufacturers', as is the case above. They were a major source of local employment.

QUEEN STREET

Above-
Queen Street taken in 2012 (SEG).

Maps of Houghton Regis prior to the late 1960s, show King Street and Queen Street, with Albert Road in the middle. Unfortunately, Albert Road no longer exists and was demolished as part of the redevelopment, of Houghton Regis.

Many streets around the country, which were built during this era, were named in honour of the immensely popular Monarchy. This is more than likely why Queen Street was thus named.

Queen Street today, has housing mainly from the Victorian period along one side. However in days gone by, Queen Street was home to a bakery, which was run by Percy Ward. One story that has emerged from local people, revolves around the Queen Street Bakery, being used to cook the Christmas Turkey (for families in the town), in the enormous Baker's Oven!

RED HOUSE COURT

Left-
The Red House
in the snow
2011 (SEG).

The Red House, which overlooks the beautiful Village Green, once formed part of the Houghton Hall Estate. The Red House, which dates back to the 18th century, has been converted into two flats, and is classed as a Grade II listed building.

The Red House is situated next to Red House Court, which comprises 33 self contained flats in an enhanced sheltered accommodation scheme. It was built in the 1991, and occupies the area where the Whitehead Foundation School was situated, and the School House. The flats were so named after its prestigious neighbour.

Left-
Red House Court
after the roof was
struck by
lightning in May
2014.
Fortunately
nobody was
injured. May
2014 (SEG).

As the picture on the previous page shows, Red House Court was struck by lightning during May 2014. The lightning, caused a fire, which well contained, but nonetheless caused a lot of damage. Residents were moved out while repairs were undertaken and fortunately nobody was injured.

RICHMOND DRIVE

Left-
A Promotional poster for 'The Parc' taken August 2010 (SEG).

Richmond Drive is on 'The Parc' Estate. It was named after Richmond Palace, which was a royal residence, built about 1501, and stands on the banks of the River Thames, in Surrey.

The Parc Estate (the building commenced in 2009), was so named by the developers, because of a 'Linear Park' (communal garden or green space), which was included in the plans for the development. The area includes some art work, and is visible from Sandringham Drive,

ROMAN GARDENS

ROMAN COURT

Roman Gardens (1975) is located off Bedford Road, which leads to the hamlet of Bidwell. It was built after Watling Court, and backs on to the area, Therefore it seems logical to think that Roman Gardens was named to continue the 'Roman' theme. Roman Court was built at a later stage, resulting in the name for the flats.

ROSLYN WAY

Above-
The picture above shows Bedford Road. Bankside Poultry Farm was located to the top left of the picture and the haystack just in front is where Roslyn Way now stands (taken during the 1930s). Reproduced by kind permission of Jon Green.

Roslyn Way stands on land formerly occupied by Mrs. Dorothy Green's arable farm. The street was named after a Roslyn, a secretary who was connected with the building company M.J Shanley. Many of the staff requested streets to be named after them, and Roslyn joined (Bob) Harrington and a lady whose surname was Plaiter, whose requests was successful.

ST JAMES CLOSE

St James Close (off Tudor Drive) was named after St James Palace in Westminster.

ST MICHAELS AVENUE

Above-
In the above picture from the 1930s, Mill Road is in the foreground, with 'Top School' to the right. Behind the trees are the first houses in St Michaels Avenue . Photo reproduced by kind permission of Jane Lousada (née Blow).

St Michaels Avenue is located off Bedford Road, opposite All Saints Parish Church. The ten yearly census returns, from 1841-1901, show Houghton Regis as being in the ecclesiastical parish 'St Michael and All Angels' as opposed to All Saints, but it is thought that this might have been a clerical error!

It has been said that the houses on St Michaels Avenue were built for the workers of AC Sphinx (later AC Delco).

St Michaels Avenue is also home to Houghton Regis Primary School. A school was located at the front of the current playing fields, facing out on to the High Street, prior to the current school being built. The school was also opposite Townsend Farm House, and was referred to as 'Top School' whereas the Whitehead Foundation School on The Green was known as 'Bottom School'.

St Michaels Avenue was an unadopted, unmade road, until the 1950s, and, when the land behind the street was developed, there were concerns that the builders might have to seek permission from the homeowners to cross the land!

SANDRINGHAM DRIVE

Above-
Sandringham Drive properties under construction in August 2010 (SEG).

Sandringham Drive was named after Sandringham House, the Norfolk retreat of the Queen. This road is neighbour to St James Close, Windsor Drive, and Kensington Close. The street was extended, with the building of 'The Parc', and there are now additional properties and streets built behind it. The Woodside Connection which is currently being constructed, will run parallel to half of Sandringham Drive and Wheatfield Road, Luton.

STUBBS CLOSE

George Stubbs (born in Liverpool 1724-1806) was known as a 'sporting painter' being famous for his pictures of horses. Owing to his studying of anatomy, it was said that his pictures were amongst the most accurate ever painted.

Stubbs Close is located on the Painters Estate and continues the theme of neighbouring streets.

TENNYSON AVENUE

Left-
Tennyson Avenue in the snow 2009 (SEG).

This street was named after Alfred Lord Tennyson who died in 1892. The street was named, following the request, from South Bedfordshire District Council, that the roads in this location be named with a royal or literary theme. The development name chosen for Milton Way and Tennyson Avenue streets was 'Houghton Hamlets'.

THE GREEN

Left-
The Memorial Hall,
The Green,
Houghton Regis,
taken in September
2012 (SEG).

'The Green' is the name given to the area, which starts at the two pairs of semi detached houses called 'The Bunch of Nuts', (bordering the Village Green on one side, taking in Houghton Hall and The Red House) and the property called 'Sunnyville' on the opposite side of the road, along to the Petrol Station opposite The Crown. The name of course comes from 'The Village Green', just opposite.

The Memorial Hall is also located on 'The Green', and the building was completed in 1953 (the foundation stone was laid by the Chairman of Luton and Rural District Council, Cllr. H.J Gale) earlier that year. Local people purchased bricks in memory of those lost during the war, and other funds were raised through village fetes and a weekly collection. The hall was intended as a building for the ex-servicemen, but unfortunately a covenant was written in to the deeds, to prohibit the hall having a permanent license to sell alcohol! This was possibly owing to previous uses for the land.

The hall has had many uses since that time, including community events, Wedding Receptions, Birthday Parties, Civic Events, Sequence Dancing, and the selection of the Houghton Regis Carnival Queen, and Princesses. The Houghton Regis Horticultural Society held an annual Summer Show at the hall for 51 years.

Houghton Regis Women's Institute has also held its meetings at the Memorial Hall since its opening. The branch itself was founded in 1945, and before the hall was

Above left-
Mrs. Mabel Stuart-Smith was the first President of the Houghton Regis W.I from 1945-1947. Photo reproduced with kind thanks to Houghton Regis W.I.

Above right-
The Houghton Regis W.I celebrates its 70th Birthday in June 2015. Councillors Chris Slough (Deputy Mayor) and Past Mayor Councillor Laura Ellaway are pictured with the members. Photo reproduced by kind thanks to Houghton Regis W.I.

built, the ladies would meet in a wooden hut in the current Memorial Hall car park.

The first President of the Houghton Regis Women's Institute in 1945, was Mrs. Mabel Stuart-Smith, who was resident at Dene Hollow, Sundon Road. Mrs. Stuart-Smith celebrated her Ruby Wedding Anniversary in 1944, and was also privileged to have taken tea at Number 10 Downing Street, (during the time of Prime Minister Harold Macmillan), with another group she was involved with, after leaving Houghton Regis for North Wales.

Today, the Houghton Regis W.I has approx. 30 members and the one of the ladies was recently invited to represent the branch at the Buckingham Palace Garden Party. The W.I are always involved in events for the town, and can be seen in the Village Green Pavilion at the Carnival and Car Show, providing tea and cakes! The group has members from many different age ranges, and, as well as being involved with craft activities, local events and fundraising, the group offers friendship and support to its members and the community.

With thanks to the Houghton Regis W.I for additional information, support and photographs.

THE LINDENS

LINDEN COURT

The name Linden comes from the Linden Tree but investigations have not shown any evidence of Linden trees on the site of this residential area.

THE VILLAGE GREEN

Left- The Millennium Memorial Stone being erected. Photo reproduced by kind permission of Houghton Regis Town Council.

The Village Green was transferred to the Parish Council in 1954, following the death of Colonel Part of Houghton Hall. There were covenants attached to this transfer, which included fireworks being prohibited.

The events held on the Village Green, following the end of the Second World War, helped to raise the funds for the Memorial Hall. Part of these Fete's included a parade, which started from 'top school' and a Fancy Dress competition. There is a Pathé News film, which shows the Fancy Dress Competition and some Barrel Racing in 1957. The winner of the Fancy Dress was Miss Tina Cheshire who was dressed as a 'Powder Puff' Girl'. The Pathé News clip also showed the Barrel Racing, which was a Houghton Regis tradition. The barrels were rolled along the High Street from the Five Bells to The Crown (the author is assured that The Five Bells was the better team!)

In late 2000, a Millennium Memorial Stone was erected on the Village Green. The stone was paid for by the fundraising activities of Town Mayor's, Councillors Pat Hamill, Mrs. Deborah Hamill and Stephen Howell. A time capsule was buried underneath and items were contributed from the local schools.

The 'Memorial Stone', as it is more commonly called, is used for the Acts of Remembrance on Remembrance Sunday and Armistice Day.

The Village Green also includes a Pavilion, which was extensively refurbished for community use in 2007.

The Village Green is still used for many public events, which include the May Fayre (re-introduced in 2013), the Carnival and the Classic Car Show (introduced in 2012). There have been many historic events held here including the Medieval Fayre (which ran from 2006-2009) and this used to attract enormous crowds. There have also been special events held to commemorate the Royal Wedding in 2011 and the Diamond Jubilee in 2012.

Above left-
Councillor Eddie Gilchrist, Town Mayor, pictured at the 2003, Houghton Regis Carnival, with thanks to Mrs. Shirley Gilchrist.

Above right-
The newly refurbished Village Green Pavilion at the re-launch in September 2007.

Left-
Councillor Robert Shimmin (Town Mayor 2015-16) at the 2015 Houghton Regis Carnival. Photos reproduced with kind thanks to Houghton Regis Town Council.

Above-

Councillor David Jones Town Mayor, (from 2012-2013) , pictured (at the head of the table) at the Diamond Jubilee Celebrations on the Village Green on a chilly day in June 2012. Councillor Jones is taking tea in the Village Green Pavilion, with guests (from left to right) Councillor Robin Hines, (Town Mayor from 2010-2011), Mrs. Mary Hines, Councillor Andrew Roberts (Town Mayor from 2011-12), and Mrs. Anne Jones, Mayoress (2012-2013). Tea was provided by the newly formed group, Houghton Regis Helpers.

Below-

Councillor Peter Williams (Town Mayor from 2013-2014) at the 2013 Carnival with representatives from Houghton Regis Academy, who won the Procession Competition. Photographs reproduced by kind permission of Houghton Regis Town Council.

Left-
Councillor Tony Swain (Town Mayor from 2008-2009) pictured at a Family History Day in September 2008, with the Coconut Shy that he introduced to raise funds for his nominated charities. (SEG).

Above-
One of the rides on the Village Green, during the visit from the Fair, taken in September 2008 (SEG).

TOWNSEND FARM ROAD

TOWNSEND TERRACE

Above-
Townsend Farm House. Photo reproduced by kind permission of Jane Lousada (née Blow).

The Industrial Estate at Townsend Farm Road was, as the name suggests, named after Townsend Farm. Townsend Furlong, as shown on the Duke of Bedford's 1762 map, was an old field name, which was located in the proximity of this farm.

The farmhouse was on the right side of High Street, if travelling from Dunstable, just passed the entrance to Mill Road. On the opposite side of the road (approximately where the industrial units, which face out on to the High Street, are located). There was a large barn, next to a large milking house. Joseph Scroggs was the owner and farmer for many years, until about 1930. After this time, Ted Huckstepp was the owner or tenant farmer of Townsend Farm from 1930 to 1950.

Joseph Scroggs was related to the Blow Family (Tithe Farm, Poynters Farm and Easthill Farm) through marriage to Leyzes Blow, sister of Farmer Ernest Garratt Blow.

Left and right-
Farmer of Townsend Farm, Joseph Scroggs.
Photos reproduced by kind permission of Jane Lousada (née Blow).

Townsend Terrace was built for the workers of the Cement Works during the 1920s. It was named owing to its location opposite Townsend Farm.

TRAVERTINE CLOSE

Left-
Travertine Close shortly after completion in 2012 (SEG).

Travertine Close forms part of the Tilia Park Estate adjacent to the quarry. Travertine is a light coloured, or white, type of calcareous rock, which is used in building. The name was chosen by Development Control at Central Bedfordshire Council, to continue the quarrying theme.

TUDOR DRIVE

Above-
Tudor Drive looking out to 'The Parc' development in March 2011 (SEG).

Tudor Drive is the road that connects Windsor Drive to Sandringham Drive. It was built during the early 1990s, and continues the royal theme. The views in this area have changed dramatically since the recent development of the land at Sandringham Drive, as the photograph above shows.

VANBRUGH DRIVE

In keeping with the rest of the Painters Estate, Vanbrugh Drive was named after dramatist and architect Sir John Vanbrugh (1664-1726) whose best known work was the design of Blenheim Palace.

WALKLEY ROAD

There is very little information available about the naming of Walkley Road, which is located at the bottom of King Street (this development took place in the 1940s).

The only place name in Britain, with that name, is in Sheffield, and the name 'Walkley' comes from the Anglo Saxon term 'Walcas Leah', meaning forest clearing. It is possible that this could have been a wooded area, before the housing was built. Maps from the 1880s show the location as being fields.

WATLING COURT

Above-
A family photo, with Mary Jane Goosey. Pictured in the centre of the front row. Photo reproduced with kind thanks to Richard Goosey.

There have been a few references made from residents about the Houghton Regis involvement in the hat industry of Luton, and census data definitely supports this.

It is known that Houghton Regis residents were employed to plait the straw from the fields, which was then sold at Dunstable Market, and also to the 'hat industry', There were many local ladies (and children) who worked plaiting the straw for the hats, and in the sewing of them.

One such lady was Mrs. Mary Jane Goosey, who was something of a Victorian business woman! Mary Jane (who was married to Alfred, and had one son called Sydney) ran her own hat business, towards the end of the 19th century, from premises beside her home on Bedford Road. This would have been quite a feat during this era. The house she owned was called 'Brooklyn Villa', which was situated on the land now occupied by Watling Court. Later Mary Jane had an identical house built next door to her own home, which was called 'Boronia'.

Above-
The picture above shows Bryan Goosey, aged 3, with his mother Nance (left) and grandmother Mary Jane Goosey, about to set out on the parade in celebration of the Coronation of George V in 1911. Behind them is Brooklyn Villa. Photo reproduced with kind permission of Richard Goosey.

Boronia was located next door to 'Ivydene', which is still standing today. Mary Jane Goosey passed away in 1927.

It is known that Ivydene (built in 1884) was once lived in by the owner of a local Lime Works (Mr. Durant and his family). It is also believed that it was once owned by a Mr. A.E Olney, who may be the Arthur Edward Olney of Olney Headwear, which has been successfully trading in Luton since 1914. The same family has

Owned Ivydene since it was sold by Mr. Olney in 1916.

Mary Jane's grandson (pictured on the previous page as a young child) worked for the Portland Cement Works and grew up in Brooklyn Villa. He also lived there as an adult with his own family, including son Richard.

Both Brooklyn Villa and Boronia were knocked down during the 1970s, and the original choice of name for Watling Court (which was built on the site of the houses and workshops) was Brooklyn Court or Brooklyn Rise. However the developers suggestion of Watling Court was taken up instead by the planning authority.

With thanks to Richard Goosey for the additional information, support and photographs.

Left-
The picture above shows beautiful 'Ivydene' decorated for the Coronation of George V (which took place on 22nd June 1911). Behind the house is the land which became St Michaels Avenue. Photo reproduced with kind thanks to Richard Goosey.

Left-
Watling Court, as viewed from the Tower of All Saints Parish Church in May 2015 (SEG).

Below-
Sydney Goosey (left in the background), in the family garden of Brooklyn Villa, with Mary Jane (2nd from right) and another couple. Ivydene is in the background. Photo reproduced with kind permission of Richard Goosey.

WATLING PLACE

According to the Council Minutes of 1967, Messrs Robinson and White built on the land, at the rear of St Michaels Avenue, which is almost certainly Watling Place. The original suggestions for the street name was Thornhill Road or Crescent, but the Parish Council objected, owing to the number of existing streets in the parish using the name 'Thorn'. It is not known from where the name for Watling Place originated, but the High Streets in Dunstable were originally called 'Watling Street' and have origins back to the Roman era. This has to be the obvious reason for the street name.

WESTBURY CLOSE

Westbury Close is situated on the Townsend Industrial Estate and comprises workshops and industrial units. The estate is located on the west side of town, which one assumes to be the reason for its name.

WHITEHOUSE CLOSE

Left-
The White House (centre of the picture). Reproduced by kind permission of the Dunstable Gazette/John Buckledee.

Whitehouse Close was built on the site of 'The White House', which stood on the High Street. The White House was once owned by Josiah Freeman (the last Miller to work the Corn Mill on the High Street (please see *Freemans Close*) and it later passed to his daughter Laura Freeman who was a Teacher at the Whitehead School, which was opposite the Village Green.

It is said that Gary Cooper spent weekends here as a boy; although, as stated earlier, it is known that he resided at 157 High Street North, whilst he was a pupil at Dunstable Grammar School. He lived at the High Street North address, with Mr. and Mrs, Barton (Emily), his mother, and brother Arthur. Emily was Laura Freeman's sister.

WHITING SQUARE

Whiting Square is located on the 'Tilia Park' Estate and 'Whiting' once again follows the quarrying theme. Incidentally, Tilia is the name given to about 30 different types of deciduous trees, including the Linden Tree and the Lime Tree, which are native to the Northern Hemisphere.

WINDSOR DRIVE

WINDSOR PLACE

Windsor Drive was named, in 1988, by the developers. It was suggested by South Bedfordshire District Council that the roads adjoining Windsor Drive be named with a royal, or literary, theme. The council considered Sandringham Drive, Glamis Drive and Edinburgh Road. The latter two were dropped. The name 'Windsor Place' was decided by the Town Council's Planning and Licensing Committee in 2002, and submitted to South Bedfordshire District Council. The Town Council tried different variations with the name Windsor in the title, before the name was finally agreed.

WOODLANDS AVENUE

Left-
Woodlands Avenue taken from the Village Green during March 2014 (SEG).

Woodlands Avenue was built by Luton and Rural District Council, and in the Town Guide of the 1950s, the following details are included about the setting…

'Due to its proximity to Luton and Dunstable, houses are much sought after in Houghton Regis, and, recognising this demand, the Rural District Council have erected a substantial number of houses in the Village. The first of these post war housing sites, ideally situated in a Woodland setting and aptly named "Woodlands Avenue", received recognition in the form of a Ministry of Health Regional Award for design and layout'.

TITHE FARM

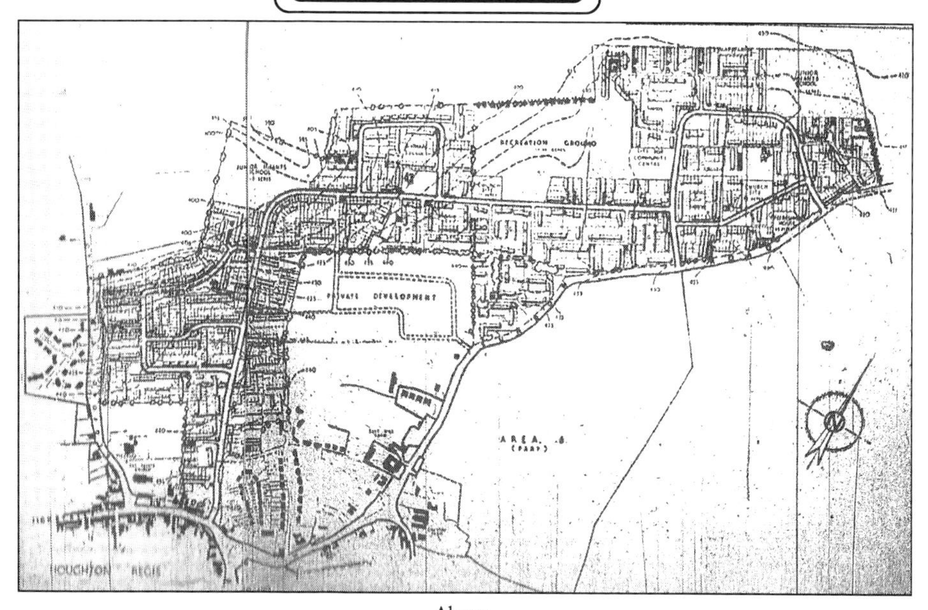

Above-
Tithe Farm Estate plan first published in the Dunstable Borough Gazette and Luton Journal, Jan1958.

The Tithe Farm Estate was built under the 'New and Expanded Towns Scheme' by Luton and Rural District Council, and caused much controversy within the village, in 1958, and beyond.

The policy of moving Londoners out of the capital, which had begun during the 1930s, was continuing, partly due to the bombing of the houses, during the Second World War (which made houses uninhabitable). Also the quality of older housing, was considered not to be of a good standard. This process, of moving the occupants, became known as 'London Overspill', and this was far more urgent in the late 1940s, following the end of the war.

As mentioned earlier, Woodlands Avenue had been successfully completed in the late 1940s, and the Parish Council subsequently were successful in securing additional council housing on the Manor Park Estate (completed in 1952/53), but housing was still in short supply. In February 1952, Luton and Rural District Council (the principal authority) approached Houghton Regis Parish Council, to ask for suggestions, as to possible housing sites, for future building. Areas that were identified, at that stage, included land opposite East Hill Farm House, and the land adjacent to the Police Houses in Park Road North. The latter became the 'Brookfield Estate'.

In August 1953, the Parish Council again approached the District Council, to enquire about its housing programme for the villages, since the Manor Park Estate was completely full. The house building had stalled, although there was still a long list of applicants.

Reports were noted in the Dunstable Gazette of 1954, that there were a few 'selected areas', which were being considered for a London Overspill housing scheme; these areas were all within a 100 mile radius of London. These first reports mentioned Dunstable as a potential location, along with nine other sites; the closest one, at that stage, being Bletchley. In February 1954, it was reported that homes were needed for some 90,000 overspill families (300,000 people), and, although Bedfordshire County Council had not made a direct approach to the London County Council, at that point, it was consulting each local authority within its (BCC's) jurisdiction (with the exception of Luton), to ascertain their views. Luton was not included in these discussions, as the town was having its development restricted under the County Plan. Luton had an overspill of its own, and Dunstable was then the 'recreational choice' for the Luton Overspill. There were financial complexities to consider, as well as the difficulties of 'cutting and pasting' families from one area to another.

The overspill scheme proposed that the 'exporting' authorities were to provide the 'importing' authorities with financial aid. It was reported that it was 'unlikely that Luton would give Dunstable any financial aid for receiving it's overspill, whereas the London County Council would be more likely to provide this financial support. However, it was felt that the Dunstable people would react better to receiving 'Lutonians' into their community, rather than Londoners. Nevertheless, it was realised that the financial aspect was something that needed further consideration. The neighbouring areas of Ampthill and Leighton Buzzard were included in the early discussions; Ampthill preferred 'Lutonians to 'Londoners' and Leighton Buzzard felt initially that they did not have enough industry to absorb any Londoners at all!

The Houghton Regis Parish Council had previously stated their wish to receive additional council housing (although ideally for their own local people). Although LRDC, and higher authorities had the final say, it was felt that local preferences were ignored (and in some cases local people were unaware of the situation through lack of consultation).

On 31st May 1955 LRDC held a public inquiry about the acquisition of land for housing development purposes, by means of Compulsory Purchase Order, and, in 1956, land owners were notified that their land was under threat. In Houghton Regis, the areas which were being considered, included the land belonging to the Smiths' of Tithe Farm (53 acres), church allotments, and land belonging to other farming families (the Andrews and the Catlings). It has been said, that the first indication to local people that their allotments were the subject of a Compulsory Purchase Order was when their agreements were not renewed.

In September 1957, the Compulsory Purchase Orders were finalised, most of the areas outlined being agreed, with very few exceptions. One house that did escape the order was 'The Hyde' on Sundon Road (only to be demolished some years later).

The 'go ahead', for the 'new town' in Houghton Regis was finally revealed in the Dunstable Borough Gazette and Luton News of January 1958. Land covering 136 acres was to be used to build 1400 houses (20% of the houses were to be two bed houses and 70% to be three beds), churches, schools and shops It was envisaged that the construction of these houses would start in Autumn 1958, and, according to the Dunstable Borough Gazette, this was 'the shape of things to come'. The first phase of the Tithe Farm Estate was officially opened in July 1959 by The Minster of Housing and Local Government Henry Brooke, together with the Chairman of Luton Rural District Council.

Many problems arose prior to, during, and following the building of this estate. Dissatisfaction with the fairness of Compulsory Purchase Orders, and inadequate compensation received, were the initial problems. Later integration proved problematic, as the local people felt that they were being 'swamped' by the incomers, and that their views, and opinions, were being ignored.

Many properties were lost on the High Street at this time. In 1964 the 14th century Tithe Barn was knocked down to make way for the Bedford Square Shopping Centre. The reason. cited for this, was its dilapidated state, which rendered it beyond repair. It has been said, on many occasions, that such demolition would not be allowed nowadays. At the end of the 1960s, Albert Road, the top section of Cumberland Street and some of King Street, was lost, and it has been suggested that some of the redevelopment was made, to encourage people to move to the new estate.

Tithe Farm hasn't been without its problems, but the community spirit is very much evident in the town, and the problems of the past, are now firmly behind it.

In the new century the town is, once again, to be increased further by decree of central government. There have been many lessons about the building of new housing and new communities, which have shaped the way that new developments are now built (and not just in bricks and mortar).

TITHE FARM WARD**

Concurrently with the Tithe Farm development of council housing, additional land was being developed by private companies. The main builder of this era (and area) was 'Mead Estates', who have constructed many of the streets, and built many of the properties, within the electoral ward. There has also been some private development in recent years.

For ease of reading, those streets, which were built later than the initial large development, but are included within the electoral ward, have been marked with ** beside the street name.

Above-
A house on the Tithe Farm Estate pictured in 1972. Photo reproduced by kind permission of the London Metropolitan Archives, City of London (ref 243504 collage.cityoflondon.gov.uk).

ALL SAINTS ROAD

Above-
A postcard from the early part of the last century featuring All Saints Parish Church.

All Saints Parish Church has stood on the same site, since the 13/14th century, and is a central point of the town's history. The street also backs on to Thomas Whitehead School, which is next to All Saints Church, and was probably built on church land.

Left-
The inside of All Saints Parish Church taken in August 2014 (SEG).

ALSOP CLOSE **

Left -
Fred Alsop in the Olympic Games.
Right-
A recent picture of Fred Alsop. Both photographs reproduced by kind permission of the Dunstable Gazette/John Buckledee.

In 1964, Luton and Rural District Council received an application from developers, Mead Estates, for the new cul-de-sac on Leafields (adjoining Long Mead) to be known as 'Renbanks'. The councillors suggested the name 'Alsop Close' after a Mr. Fred Alsop of Leafields, Houghton Regis - to commemorate his recent selection for the British Olympic Team. It is believed that Mr. Alsop took part in the 'Hop, Skip and Jump' event, which is now called the 'Triple Jump'.

ANGELS LANE

Local people used to call the footpath which ran between All Saints Church and the National School (now home to 20, 21 and 22 Bedford Square) 'Angels Lane'. The name certainly dates back to at least the 1920s and it is thought that the name was taken from the large angel statue, which stands in All Saints Churchyard, marking the grave of Martha Bowler who died in 1879 aged 72 years.

Left-
Photograph of the angel statue on the grave of Martha Bowler taken in October 2014 (SEG).

According to the Dunstable Borough Gazette of 30th January 1959, the streets in Tithe Farm were named after the English countryside. Originally, the streets were to be named First, Second etc. with Tithe Farm Road being called 'Broadway'. Other suggestions for names on Tithe Farm, suggested by Councillor T.J Strange were Dove Close, Cherry Close and Stranges' Folly! (incidentally there was a Cllr. Cherry and Cllr. Dove). These names however did not win any support with the Parish Council, and so the English countryside names (mainly trees and hedgerows) were adopted.

BEDFORD SQUARE

Left- The Brownies and Guides celebrate the Coronation of Queen Elizabeth II in the National Schoolrooms. The building was pulled down prior to the shops being built. Photo reproduced with kind thanks to Mary Sidgwick (née Holt).

Bedford Square Shopping Centre was opened on 24th September 1966, and comprises retail units, the Library, Health Centre, and split level maisonettes.

The centre was built by Hammerson Properties and Investments Limited (the company behind Brent Cross Shopping Centre and the new Bullring Shopping Centre, in Birmingham). For a while, the centre was owned by C.I.N Properties, who later became the Coal Miners Pension Board. The centre was designed to provide the village with its own facilities, following the increase in population, as a result of the London Overspill. The square is a typical example of 1960s architecture, and is similar to both the Purley Centre and Dominic Square, which are shopping precincts of the same era, in Luton.

The Council Minutes. on 4th January 1966, record that there were four possible suggestions for the name of the new shopping precinct. These were: Regis Green Precinct; Green Regis Precinct; Green Royal Precinct; and Royal Green Precinct. None of those names was actually chosen!

It is most likely that the name Bedford Square derives from the Russell Family, who are the Dukes of Bedford. The family owned land around Russell Square in London, one such street being named 'Bedford Square'. The Duke of Bedford was also one time Lord of the Manor of Houghton Regis.

The centre was officially opened by the comedy actress, Hattie Jacques, who was known for her roles in the 'Carry On' Films. She had been chosen, owing to her ability to identify with a wide audience, and due to the fact that that many of the population of Houghton Regis were London Overspill. Photographs of the opening ceremony show a group of Morris Dancers outside where Roger Marsh and Co is now situated. On the wall, behind the dancers, is an emblem, or coat of arms, and readers may note the indentations of a shield, still visible today, on the black painted area. This is believed to be the eagle of Barclays Bank, which was the first tenant of no.9 Bedford Square (indeed the bank vaults still run underneath this property).

Left- Bedford Square Shopping Centre pictured in the 1990s. Photo reproduced by kind permission of Houghton Regis Town Council.

Many people remember shops and stores which used to occupy the centre, e.g. Bunces Newsagents, Greaves and Tompkins Estate Agents, Bishops Supermarket and Widdisons the Chemists. There are many more, which have appeared, and then disappeared over the years.

Natwest opened its branch in Bedford Square in 2002, following a successful campaign. The opening was covered on the local television news and made the national press.

Left-
The Natwest Jazz Band performing at the opening of the Bank in June 2002 (SEG).

Below-
Bedford Square in 2003 (SEG).
Right-
Natwest balloons handed out in Bedford Square taken at the opening of the branch in 2002 (SEG).

Left-
The original Houghton Regis Library in 1972. Photo reproduced by kind permission of the London Metropolitan Archives, City of London (ref 243816 collage.cityof london.gov.uk).

Left-
Councillor Mrs. Lynda Walmsley (Town Mayor from 2009-2010) on 1st September 2009, in the new Houghton Regis Library, just prior to its opening (SEG).

Left-
The Manager of Natwest, Samantha, presents a cheque in sponsorship of the 2003 Houghton Regis Carnival to Councillor Eddie Gilchrist (Town Mayor 2003-2004) with Councillor Mrs. Shirley Gilchrist and Regis the Lion. Photo reproduced by kind permission of Houghton Regis Town Council.

The Shopping Centre and Library were extensively refurbished (work commencing in late 2007, being completed in Autumn 2009). The project included a brand new Library and Health Centre, which replaced the outdated facilities, built in the 60s. The refurbishments included repaving the Shopping Centre which improved its aesthetic appearance. The Community Centre was also extensively refurbished.

BRAMBLES EDGE**

Left-
Newly completed houses on Brambles Edge (2013) SEG.

This was the name given, in 2008, to the houses built on the area formerly occupied by a bungalow called 'The Firs' on East End. The name was given to remain within the shrub/tree theme. Unfortunately, in 2011, the houses, although named, had not been built! This caused some chaos with the post and circulars, which had been sent out to non existent properties. The private development built by Bellcross Homes was completed during 2014.

BORDERS WAY

Before the modern day developments took place, most of Houghton Regis was divided up into farms, fields and furlongs. One such field was 'The Borders' which is the likely origin of 'Borders Way'.

CAMP DRIVE

Above-
Postcard of the Village Green showing soldiers on parade on the Village Green, during the time of the First World War.

It is widely believed that Camp Drive was named in honour of the Army Regiment which occupied the Village Green, and land, behind Tithe Farm, during the First World War.

Documents, in the possession of the Town Council, have shown that the Village Green was taken by Order of Whitehall, during the First World War, with the guarantee that the land was restored to its former condition at the end of the conflict. It is said however that in certain parts of The Green, it is still possible to see indentations, caused by the pitching of the tents!

CHURCHFIELD ROAD

Left-
Photograph of the 'new' houses along Churchfield Road and the corner of All Saints Road.
Photo reproduced by kind permission of the London Metropolitan Archives, City of London (1959) (ref: 243728 collage.city oflondon.gov.uk).

This road not only owes its name to its actual location behind All Saints Parish Church, but also to the fact that the land, now known as Churchfield Road, was probably the same piece of land, noted on the Duke of Bedford's 1762 map as 'Church Field'. Beside it was an area called Church Hill. There were also allotments in Houghton Regis known by the name of 'Churchfield Allotments', which were sold under a Compulsory Purchase Order in 1957.

CROSSWAYS**

Crossways is a private development, built on land off Sundon Road. A number of names were suggested for this road, and these included:

- Pond's Way (after the pond on the corner of Sundon Road).
- St George's Close (a companion to St Andrews Lane).
- Sundon Close.
- Crossways.
- Warren Close (possibly after the surname of one of the homeowners on Sundon Road).

It seems logical that Crossways was suggested, owing to it's location at the cross roads of Sundon Road, Park Road North, Parkside Drive and East End.

DALLING DRIVE**

Dalling Drive
March 2015
(SEG).

Whilst writing for the 'Town Crier Newsletter' on behalf of the Town Council, I included an invitation to residents to let me know if they had any information, regarding the naming of their street. I was delighted when I received a letter, from Mrs. Carpenter, of Dalling Drive, telling me about this unusual name.

The story went that one of the first people to move in to the road was a Mr. and Mrs. Smith, and when this resident was putting down a deposit with the builders, it was noted that Mrs. Smith had recently changed from her maiden name of Dalling to her married name of Smith. The builders (Mead Estates Ltd) then proclaimed that they would call the street after her! The Parish Council requested that the original suggestion of Dalling Walk be changed to 'Dalling Drive'.

DELL ROAD

DELLMONT ROAD

"The Dell' and 'Dell Piece' were both situated on land to the right of Bedford Road, as shown the Duke of Bedford's 1762 map of Houghton Regis. It seems very likely that the street names have come from these old field names.

Dell Farm was located in Bidwell, and there was a house, called Dell Mount, which stood on the land now occupied by the Plymouth Brethren Church. Dell Farm was reportedly one of the largest breeders of Aylesbury Ducks in the country.

DRURY LANE**

It was rumoured that Drury Lane was given it's name by the troops, (mainly from London), who were stationed there, during the First World War. However Drury Lane is noted on census returns, which predates the First World War, and sadly seems to dispel this theory. The oldest property on Drury Lane is said to date back to the 16th century, and was lived in by Charlotte Hudson (Laundress) in 1901.

EASTHILL ROAD **

Left-
The rear of East Hill Farm House. Photograph reproduced by kind permission of Mr. A. Hemmings.

Easthill Road is named after Easthill Farm. The farm was located on Sundon Road (formerly called Chalton Road), and it was shown on the Duke of Bedford's 1762 map of Houghton Regis. The farmhouse is Georgian, and could have been built anytime between the start of the Georgian era in 1714 and the production of the map in 1762. Easthill Farmhouse, which is Grade II listed, is still standing today, and stands on 0.81 of an acre of land. It has only changed hands twice during the 20th century!

It is known that Easthill Farm was farmed by the Cook family, which is evidenced by the 1901 census. The other recorded owner was Mr. Leonard Jack Blow, who purchased the farm during the 1930s. Leonard was no stranger to farming, as his parents Ernest Garratt Blow and Lucy Lily Blow (née Waterfield) were the farmers at Tithe Farm (where Leonard was born in 1913), before moving to Poynters Farm. Leonard had one brother Ernest Lynton Blow. Lucy Blow died in 1933 and Ernest in 1940. Lucy is buried in All Saints Churchyard.

The land for the first houses on the 'Easthill Estate' was sold by (Leonard) Jack Blow (also known as John) in June 1938, presumably for the immediate building of houses. A further transfer of land was made in October 1938, which indicates that this might have been from the builders to the first owners.

Above-
An aerial photograph of Sundon Road, with the area soon to be known as 'Easthill Road' in view to the right. Photo reproduced by kind permission of Jane Lousada (née Blow).

Above-
The front of Easthill Farm House in the 1940s /1950s.Photo reproduced by kind permission of Jane Lousada (née Blow).

Above-
Leonard (Jack) Blow, pictured with Richard Goosey, Iris Blow and Frances Goosey in the 1950s. Photo reproduced by kind permission of Jane Lousada (née Blow).

Above-
Jane Blow from Easthill Farm on a May Day Float in 1954 / 1955. Photo reproduced by kind permission of Jane Lousada (née Blow).

Initially, Easthill Road was a cul-de-sac, and it is possible to see which houses were original, by the change in style, as the street was extended. Originally there were four pairs of semi detached houses, on the left hand side of the road, and at the end of the cul-de-sac was the 'Cooking Depot', which was used during the Second World War.

In some areas, these depots were used as a communal kitchen for people whose homes had been bombed, had run out of ration coupons, or otherwise needed help (Luton was extensively affected during the Second World War). In Houghton Regis, the Ministry of Food's Cooking Depot was opened around July/August 1942, and was operated by the Women's Voluntary Service (WVS), who distributed pies and supplied hot meals. Some of the pies were distributed to agricultural workers, under a special scheme. In 1945 the Houghton Regis Depot averaged 7,800 meals per week and was managed by Luton and Rural District Council's Special Services Committee.

Cllr. Robin Hines, remembers the Cooking Depot. The building was white in colour, with black chimneys on top, and was situated almost at a right angle to the road (slightly off-set to the left). The inside was filled with large ovens. Cllr. Hines remembers a walk from the Cooking Depot to Cumberland Street, transporting some prunes and custard, by means of an old fashioned pram. These needed warming up, when he arrived home! Cllr. Hines believes that it may have been a practise run, or possibly because his family had soldiers billeted with them. The depot was recorded as being disused, during the 1950s, being demolished sometime later.

The Luton News of 11th February 1954 reported that Mr. Blow of Easthill Farm had been excavating his land over the past two years, and had found evidence of a Roman building, plus pottery, dating from the time of King Alfred! Mr. Blow, in his spare time, had been digging several acres in the north eastern extremity of the village, which formed part of Easthill Farm. The story about his interesting finds has been included in this book (as shown in the newspaper article featured on page 90).

Documentation held by Central Bedfordshire Council, shows correspondence between Mr. Blow and a Mr. Freeman who was the Curator of the British Museum, detailing some of his finds. Mr. Blow reportedly made his first finds of ancient material during 1938, and this material was preserved, but no further organised investigations were started until early 1952, when a stone pavement in the garden of Easthill Farm was found. One of Mr. Blow's finds included a skeleton believed to be that of a lady of about 5ft 3" in height, who was found between two Ovid pits. Some of Mr. Blow's finds were placed on display in the Luton Museum.

With thanks to Jane Lousada (née Blow) for additional information, support and photographs.

HE DUG UP HISTORY ON HIS FARM

EVIDENCE of a Roman building, and pottery of King Alfred's day, are among the discoveries made by Mr. L. J. Blow, of Easthill Farm Houghton Regis, digging by himself in his spare time during the past two years.

He has excavated a site of several acres in the north-eastern extremity of the present village which forms part of the farm.

Houghton Regis was a Royal Manor before the Norman Conquest, and for a long time this site has been considered the probable site of the Saxon village. "It is not known when the village became Royal property, but it is known that Houghton Regis was an old-established village before the town of Dunstable was created," Mr. Blow says.

On the site under excavation, the earliest occupation so far discovered is of the Roman period, and coins, pottery and barrel locks have been found.

The barrel locks are now in Luton Museum, and are thought to be the only specimens so far discovered in Bedfordshire.

There is also evidence of a Roman building, possibly of the villa type, which it is hoped to trace if it has not been obliterated.

ST. NEOTS WARE

By about the time of King Alfred, the area flourished, and from this period comes a good deal of St. Neots ware, a well-made pottery rarely found in Bedfordshire. Much slag and iron ore has been found, and appears to be of the same period.

No remains of furnaces havr been recognised so far, but iron ore was certainly smelted here in some quantity. Mr. Blow says: "Analysis of some of the slag shows that a primitive and wasteful system of smelting was employed, and although this would produce a very pure iron, the soft nature of the metal is evidenced by the large number of whetstones discovered."

Parts of a number of band mills made of volcanic lava have been identified by Professor Roder, of Koblenz, as coming from Mayen in the Rhineland.

"Handmills of this material are rare and, one would have thought, less suitable than those made of native stone," says Mr. Blow.

Digging has revealed a number of pits of peculiar shape, and the skull of a small ox of the "Highland Cattle" type was found in one of them.

A great deal of pottery of the 11th and 12th centuries has been found, but there is a marked absence of later material. The area seems to have been deserted in the 13th century, perhaps owing to some change in the agricultural system.

The abandonment appears to have taken place well before the Black Death, but it is possible this, or an earlier plague, was responsible.

Mr Blow says the small area so far examined is insignificant compared with the area of the settlement, but the site promises other discoveries, and it is hoped to carry out further excavations.

"In view of the area involved I would welcome assistance in the hope of elucidating more of the history of the parish during a period of which little is known," he adds.

Left-
The original article from the Luton News from February 1954. Reproduced with kind thanks from the Luton News.

EDDIWICK AVENUE

Houghton Regis was home to many fields, and the Duke of Bedford's 1762 map show that the fields were all divided into separate furlongs. There is a mention of Lower Eddiwick Furlong and Short Eddiwick Furlong, which were located approximately where Eddiwick Avenue is today.

FARM CLOSE**

The developers 'Mead Estates Ltd' suggested the name 'Farm Close' and the connection surely lies with Easthill Farm. Farm Close is located off Easthill Road, and on land which formerly belonged to the farm.

GABLE WAY

The term gable relates to a part of a building, and in particular roofs. A gable is the triangle portion between the edges of a sloping roof. However it is not clear as to why this should have been applied to this road.

GRASMERE WALK

Unfortunately there are no minutes regarding the naming of this road. Most of the streets on the Tithe Farm Estate have been named after the countryside, but it is recorded that a Mr. Roberts, of Kensworth, suggested names for some of the roads. It is not known which ones he suggested, or if they were ever taken up! Possibly he had fond memories of holidays in the Lake District.

GROVE ROAD

The word 'grove' means a small wood or plantation, and may have been chosen to reflect the countryside/tree/shrub theme of the estate. There is a Grove Farm, in Houghton Regis, but this is located off Bedford Road.

HAYLEY COURT **

Hayley Court was built by Mead Estates Ltd, the building firm started by William Mead. It has been said that this area was once designated for tennis courts!

It was said that the original name for 'Hayley Court' was 'Haylot Court', which was a farming term, denoting the fact that the area was surrounded by farms. Unfortunately, it is believed that the Parish Council refused the name owing to its similarity to the word 'Harlot'!

HILLBOROUGH CRESCENT

Left-
Shops at Hillborough Crescent all dressed up during the Football World Cup June 2010 (SEG).

Hillborough Crescent was the second road to be built on the new Tithe Farm Estate. The original name for this subsidiary road was Hilbury Crescent, but, by 1960, the name was changed to Hillborough. It is likely that the name comes from Long Hillborough Furlong and Short Hillborough Furlong, which are shown on the 1762 Duke of Bedford's map.

One business, which has been situated in Hillborough Crescent, for many years, is the Nisa store (previously known as Londis). In 2010, the then owners, Kishor and Pat Patel, celebrated their 25th anniversary in the shop, at the Houghton Regis Carnival, with a special Birthday Cake! The cake was so large, that it was placed on a door! It was cut by Margaret Atkins, who had been employed at the store for very many years, and the cake was served to the public at the Carnival.

Left-
Town Mayor, Cllr Robin Hines with Margaret Atkins of Nisa and owner Kishor Patel, cutting the cake at the Carnival, taken in July 2010 reproduced by kind permission of Houghton Regis Town Council.

Left-
The Nisa Smart Car with Carnival Mascot 'Regis The Lion' at the 2010 Carnival. reproduced by kind permission of Houghton Regis Town Council.

HILLSIDE

This road, backing onto Bedford Road, was almost certainly a literal name, because of its location.

KENT ROAD

KENTWICK SQUARE

Kent Road may have origins with the London Overspill population, and Kentwick Square may be an amalgamation of Kent and Eddiwick, and the road is also in the form of a perfect square!

LEAFIELDS **

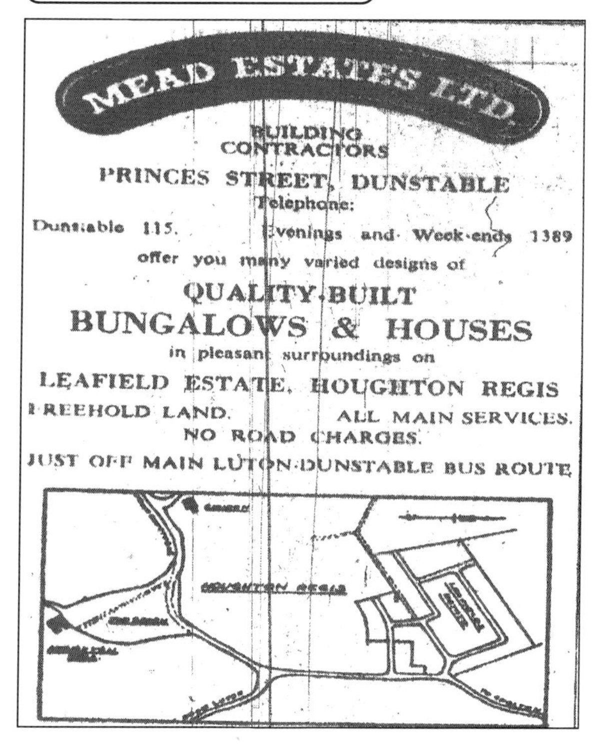

Left-
An advert by Mead Estates in 1958 for the houses and bungalows on Leafields. Reproduced by kind permission of the Dunstable Gazette / Luton News.

The properties on Leafields were built by Mead Estates Ltd, and the road was named by them in 1955. The estate was originally classed as being built at Chalton Road, which was the original name for Sundon Road. The area occupied by Leafields was once farmland belonging to Easthill Farm, and is likely just to be a literal name, relating to the fields, and the River Lea, which runs nearby. The name was suggested by the Parish Council, with 'odds on one side and evens on the other', 'to avoid confusion'. An advert by the builder's in 1959, describes the properties as the 'latest in modern styling', and as 'modern as the minute'.

One house which stands on Leafields, was definitely as 'modern as the minute', but it was not designed by Meads! Number 157 Leafields was built slightly later and is of a completely different style from that of its neighbours. One reason for this, is that the property is suggested as being an ex Ideal Home Exhibition house, built from an individual plan, and it is said to be completely unique!

Left- Leafields in 1972. Reproduced by kind permission of the London Metropolitan Archives, City of London (ref 243793 collage.cityoflondon.gov.uk).

Left- The individually designed house on Leafields, with kind thanks to Eric and Jenny Gallucci. July 2015.

The house (originally known as plot 157), was originally owned jointly by Ronald Holmes (who acquired the plot in 1959) and Mead Estates. Mr. Holmes owned the finished property until 1965. It is known that the house next door, number 159, was originally the Leafields show home.

With thanks to Eric and Jenny Gallucci for their support, additional information and photograph.

LONG MEAD **

Long Mead forms part of the original Tithe Farm Estate, and Alsop Close, (a private development by Mead Estates), was later built to the rear of this. The actual reasons for the name of this road is not absolutely clear, but one could suggest that it may have been named, owing to its proximity to the streets built by Mead Estates.

MEADS CLOSE**

The name 'Meads Close' was suggested by the Parish Council and presumably was based on the surname of the company who built it.

PARK AVENUE**

Park Avenue is likely to be a literal name for the cul-de-sac opposite the Village Green. There are three cottages called 'Park Cottages' which are located on the corner of Drury Lane. These were built for the workers at Houghton Hall.

PEEL STREET

According to the Dunstable Gazette of January 30th 1959, an original suggestion for Peel Street, was Coppers Walk! This is because two police houses were due to be built on the street, and it was thought that it may be helpful to strangers in the area, who might wish to find the local constabulary The name however, did not win any support! Peel Street was one of the first streets on the Tithe Farm Estate to be occupied, and one of the first families to move in was the Rowe family.

Left-
Town Council Offices on Peel Street in 2009. Photo reproduced by kind permission of Houghton Regis Town Council.

Left-
Town Mayor, Councillor David Hill, and Deputy Mayor, Councillor Eddie Gilchrist take tea with Father Jonathan Redvers-Harris from All Saints Parish Church in the Mayor's Office. Jan 2003 (SEG).

The Council Offices have been located in Peel Street since 1976, but the building is known to many as the Doctor's Surgery, which was its previous use. The office is an extended 'Portacabin' with brick built outer walls, but, considering its temporary structure, it is in remarkably good condition! From the mid 1980s to 2006, the Town Council Office building was also home to the South Bedfordshire District Council Area Cash Office, where many local people visited to pay rent, and Council Tax.

The Cash Office was located at the front of the building, facing the blocked paved area in the picture, but was closed by the District Council, as a budget saving measure. The area is now occupied by offices and meeting facilities for the Town Council.

RECREATION ROAD

Left-
Tithe Farm Recreation Ground pictured at the occasion of the opening of the Skate Park in July 2009. Photograph reproduced by kind permission of Houghton Regis Town Council.

There is nothing in the official records about the naming of Recreation Road, but, with its proximity to the Tithe Farm Recreation Ground (directly opposite), this, almost certainly, is the reason for its name. The Tithe Farm Recreation Ground was officially opened on 19th July 1972 and now boasts a pavilion, football pitches, children's play equipment, a Multi Use Games Area, and a Skate Park.

ST ANDREWS LANE**

ST DAVIDS WAY

In 1965, the extension to Easthill Road, on the Leafields Estate, had recently been completed, but local residents complained that confusion was caused by its similarity to the pre-existing East Hill Lane. A petition was submitted to Luton and Rural District Council on the issue, and the resolution of this matter was to rename 'East Hill Lane' as 'St Andrews Lane'.

St Davids Way, forms part of the Tithe Farm Estate. There are no details recorded in the minutes as to why it was chosen, but St David is, of course, the Patron Saint of Wales. St Georges Close was one of the original suggestions for Crossways and St Andrews Lane followed in 1965. St Andrews Lane was originally called 'East Hill Lane' and was renamed following permission from the owner of 'St Andrews' in Sundon Road. It is reasonable to assume that the intention was to name them after the Patron Saints of the United Kingdom, St David's being the first one of the four. To date there is still no St Patrick or St George!

SCHOOL WALK

School Walk was almost certainly named because it leads from Hillborough Crescent to Grove Road, where Thornhill Lower School is located.

SHORT PATH

It would appear that the reason behind the naming of Short Path is quite literal! Short Path is situated between Tithe Farm Road and Leaf Road.

SUNDON ROAD

Above-
Sundon Road in an early postcard dating back to the time of the First World War.

Sundon Road runs from The Chequers Public House to 'Chalton Cross' and forms part of the 'Tithe Farm Estate'. There was some confusion about whether the road was actually called Chalton Road or Sundon Road, Luton and Rural District Council being asked for their confirmation on this. In the end, the Parish Council were asked to vote on the road name, and Sundon Road won this by a majority vote of just one!

The picture on the previous page shows one of the ponds which was situated at the junction of East End and the corner of Sundon Road. The area is now surrounded by willow trees. According to 'Old Houghton Regis' by Don Rowe, the little girl in the picture is Rene Smith, and her brother, Tom. He is the little boy who is leaning over the railings. Rene and Tom moved to Houghton Regis just before the outbreak of the First World War, and their father worked for Colonel Part (who was the owner of Houghton Hall, at that time) operating the electricity generator. The family lived in one of the Park Cottages; all three of these cottages were occupied by workers of Houghton Hall.

Sundon Road is fortunate to have both Dene Hollow and Easthill Farmhouse, which are both Grade II listed properties. In addition, houses 21-23 Sundon Road were built in 1848 by the Duke of Bedford, as workers cottages.

Above-
Sundon Road Police Station taken in April 2015 (SEG).

Sundon Road is also home to Houghton Regis Police Station, which was built during the 1960s. Previously the Luton and Rural District Council Offices (later becoming South Bedfordshire District Council Offices) were located opposite, on land now occupied by Hammersmith Close.

The Harvest Home Public House is also on the corner of Sundon Road and Hillborough Crescent, and it celebrated its 50th Anniversary in November 2013.

THE CLOISTERS

The name 'Cloisters' has monastic origins, but why this name was chosen for this street name is unclear. The name 'cloisters', relates to a covered walk, with an open colonnade on one side, running along the walls of buildings forming a quadrangle. This again has little relevance to the street name, although it is on one side (of a quadrangle) with Tithe Farm Road and Sycamore Road.

The original suggested names for this road were The Cloisters, The Priory and The Covey.

THE HYDE**

Although technically in the Parkside electoral ward, the flats, called 'The Hyde', are located on Sundon Road. They were built on the site of a large detached house having been called 'The Hyde', former home of local writer George Jackson. The house was saved from the 1957 Compulsory Purchase Order, but was sold to the District Council in the 1970s. It was used to house tenants until it was knocked down to build the flats.

According to 'From Countryboy to Weatherman' written by George Jackson, 'The Hyde' was named after the field where it was built. This was called 'Little Hyde'.

THE LINK

The Link is probably a literal name as it links Tithe Farm Road to Long Mead.

THE QUADRANT**

The Quadrant was built by Mead Estates and was literally named.

THORNBURY COURT**

Thornbury was the original name for the Manor House in Houghton Regis.

THORNHILL CLOSE**

Thornhill Close is a more modern street, which runs around the back of Thornhill School. It has recently come to light, that this part of the Tithe Farm Development was named 'Thornhill Estate', and that, again, may be a literal name.

THORNVIEW ROAD

Thornview Road is located between Churchfield Road and Bedford Road, which leads to the hamlet of Thorn. Therefore the reasoning behind this street name seems to be literal, as there is a good view of the countryside from Churchfield Road.

TITHE FARM ROAD

Above-
A photograph taken circa 1910 taken at Tithe Farm.

It is known that the name for the main street in the estate comes from Tithe Farm with the 15th century Tithe Barn, which was located on what is now 'Tithe Farm Road'.

A Tithe Barn was used in the middle ages to store 'tithes'. Ten percent of a farm's produce which had to be given to the church. The original plan was to try and incorporate the barn into the new street framework, but unfortunately it was pulled down for safety reasons. The barn was situated where Bedford Square is now cited, on Tithe Farm Road.

Tithe Farm changed hands many times and in the space of about 100 years, was owned by the Scroggs, the Coopers (1860s), the Blows (see *Easthill Road)* and latterly the Smiths, who were their last owners during the 1950s. The postcard above, from the early part of the last century, shows Tithe Farm House on the right of the picture, behind the two figures.

As mentioned previously, the building of the Tithe Farm Estate was met with much controversy within the village.

Above-
A postcard from the early 1900s, showing the area known as 'The Green', looking towards the High Street and Tithe Farm. The Tithe Barn can be seen to the right of the picture.

The decisions made regarding the Overspill Estates, were taken at county level, as opposed to, directly, by the parishes and towns involved. It seems that most of the decision making was taken out of local councils' hands. There is certainly little that was recorded by the Parish Council, except to read and note reports taken by higher authorities. The subject of large scale building, though, was something which was happening all over the country, following the end of the Second World War. Houghton Regis was affected dramatically by this.

Following the decision, that the estate was to go ahead, Parish Councillors visited another similar estate, in order to view the style of housing that was planned for the area. The building commenced during the latter part of 1958.

The plans for the Tithe Farm Estate comprised 1400 properties, and it is said that the population 'almost doubled overnight'. The houses were built to a good standard, with front and back gardens, garages in some cases, and good sized rooms. Houghton Regis was also close to Vauxhall Motors in Luton, which was a major employer at that time. This provided immediate employment for the new residents.

Above-
An example of a newly built terrace on Tithe Farm Road, in 1959. Reproduced by kind permission of the London Metropolitan Archives, City of London (ref 243733 collage.cityoflondon.gov.uk).

The Tithe Farm Estate was formally opened in 1959 by the minister for Housing and Local Government. However it was reported that the Chairman of Luton and Rural District Council made no reference to the Parish Council, (presumably in a speech), which did not go down well with members! This perhaps clearly demonstrates the situation.

Prior to the Tithe Farm Estate being built, the Parish Council was investigating the possibility of an area of public open space to be used for recreational purposes. The Rural District Council advised the Parish Council that plans for this should be placed on the back burners, owing to the new developments, presumably so that something could be incorporated within the plans. The area of open space was realised, and that area is the 'Tithe Farm Recreation Ground'.

As well as schools and new shopping facilities, the estate included a new church. The original St Vincent's Church, was located on Tithe Farm Road, on land adjacent to Tithe Farm Recreation Ground. The church was erected during the late 1960s, and, in addition to worship, was used for Bingo, exercise sessions and social events, including Wedding Receptions.

Above-
St Vincent's Church pictured in the mid 1990s on the land adjacent to Tithe Farm Recreation Ground.
Photograph reproduced by kind permission of Houghton Regis Town Council.

A new church for St Vincent's was built on the Parkside Estate, and unfortunately, over time, the old building fell into disrepair. It was decided in 1996 that it should be sold. Sadly the premises fell victim to arson shortly afterwards, and the land has stood vacant ever since. Many local people have fond memories of the church and hall, and were sad to see it disappear.

Over the past 50 years, the Tithe Farm Estate has become integrated into the town, and much has now moved into private ownership.

VICARAGE ROAD

Above-
Vicarage Road in 1959. Photo Reproduced by kind permission of the London Metropolitan Archives, City of London (ref: 243729 collage.cityoflondon.gov.uk).

It seems almost certain that Vicarage Road was named after the Vicarage of All Saints Parish Church, which is adjacent to the road.

PARKSIDE

Above-
An aerial photograph taken on 1st July 1968 showing the border of Houghton Regis with Luton (to the bottom right and the Tithe Farm Estate in the top left) The large undeveloped area to the right of the centre is 'Area 5', later to become the Parkside Estate and an extension to the Houghton Hall ward. Photo reproduced with kind permission of Central Bedfordshire Council©.

The Parkside Estate is located to the east of the town, and was added to Houghton Regis in the early 1970s, as a mixture of private and social housing, with the latter being built by the Greater London Council.

Following the completion of the Tithe Farm Estate, attention was drawn to the potential development of an area known as 'Area 5' (under the Town Development Act 1952). This 'Area' had been shown on maps dating from the time that the Tithe Farm Estate was planned, and comprised some of the area taken under the Compulsory Purchase Orders of the 1950s.

However the Parish Council had changed its view, after the large increase in population, only six years previously, and objected to the proposed plans for 'Area 5' . One of the reasons noted in the minute book was that 'it was too near to London' and that some families had already returned and others still worked in London'. In June 1965 the Parish Council was told that the area had been allocated in the Luton and Dunstable Town Map, approved by the Ministry of Housing and Local Government, some years earlier, and that the Parish Council had not objected at that time! The Ministry of Housing and Local Government visited, in order to meet with councillors from Bedfordshire County Council and Luton and Rural District Council.

In a shared venture between the Greater London Council, Bedfordshire County and Luton and Rural District Council, the first 271 houses were built in 1970, on Parkside Drive, Enfield Close, Brentwood Close and Elm Park Close. The name 'Parkside' was chosen for the estate, to reflect its location on the edge of the Houghton Hall parkland.

The scheme was built under the 'Radburn System', Radburn being the name of the architect who created estates with housing areas, designed to keep pedestrians and vehicles apart! Many schemes in America have been built under this system, and local examples include Milton Keynes and Marsh Farm. The main principals of the Radburn System are to build long avenue type main roads for the cars, and inner facing housing areas for the safety of pedestrians. Streets could be accessed through underpasses, and houses were built with garages in blocks. The houses themselves were built back to front, to permit parking areas at the rear. It was designed with safety in mind. The Parkside Estate was officially opened in August 1971 and it is reported that the new estate was visited by the then Junior MP, Michael Heseltine, later Lord Heseltine.

The 'private' section of Parkside was started during the early 1970s and was built by M.J Shanley. The name of the development was called the 'Houghton Park Estate', although there was no actual parkland in this area; most of the estate being built on land which once belonged to Poynters Farm.

Hawthorn Park School, was opened in 1973, as a new Primary School for the estate. The school has recently become a Community Primary School and now has in the region of 400 pupils from the area. There is also a Day Centre on Parkside Drive, which was opened in 1976.

Community Development within Parkside, from the very outset was extremely important. In 1978 South Bedfordshire District Council opened a 'Friendship House' on Chelsea Gardens, which was used as a means of alleviating social isolation for some of the new families, who had relocated to the town. The House was used to host coffee mornings and playgroups, remaining open until the late 1980s.

Additional housing was added in this area, during the early 1980s, with the Barratt's Estate In 1984, the Dog and Duck Public House was built on Parkside, as a facility for the new residents, as was the Parkside Drive Recreation Ground.

During the 1990s it was revealed that many of the houses built by the GLC were suffering from some building defects. South Bedfordshire District Council had a large task in rectifying the problems, the resulting cost running into several hundred thousand pounds. Thankfully the affected houses were repaired, and there has been no repeat of these concerns.

For many years, the annual Carnival Procession has left from Parkside. Initially this was from the Parkside Drive Recreation Ground, but since 2011, it has left from Houghton Regis Academy, (formerly known as Kings Houghton Middle School).

Above left-
Mosaic outside Hawthorn Park School.
Taken June 2015 (SEG).

Above right-
One of the Mosaics inside the school, designed by Sian Hall and Adam Barker during the early 1990s.
Taken June 2015 (SEG).

ABBEY WALK

Abbey Walk (1971) was originally to be called Friars Walk but owing to a road of the same name in Dunstable, the Head Postmaster raised an objection! Abbey Walk was suggested in its place; but unfortunately no reason for the name of this street was given.

ASHWELL WALK

THERFIELD WALK

Left-
Chantry Cottage in the Village of Ashwell, Hertfordshire. Photo reproduced by kind permission of Ashwell Village Museum, with thanks to Ashwell Parish Council.

Unfortunately, there are no details listed in the council minutes about the naming of Ashwell Walk, or Therfield Walk, on the Houghton Park Estate. However, both Ashwell and Therfield are both places names for villages, about six miles apart, near Royston, Hertfordshire.

Ashwell is an Anglo-Saxon Market Town, mentioned in the Domesday Book, with its own Horticultural Society and Women's Institute. There is also a cottage called 'Chantry Cottage'. Houghton Regis also has Saxon origins, is mentioned the Domesday Book, has similar clubs and societies, and was home to Chantry House and Farm. This could be all coincidental, but there are some similarities to Houghton Regis!

Therfield has three 'Green's' and interestingly a pub called 'The Fox and Duck'.

BLOOMSBURY GARDENS

BRENTWOOD CLOSE

BROMLEY GARDENS

CHELSEA GARDENS

Left- Brentwood Close in 1972. Picture reproduced by kind permission of the London Metropolitan Archives, City of London (ref: 243824) collage.cityoflondon.gov.uk).

The meeting of the Houghton Regis Parish Council in December 1973, chaired by S.C. Clarke (MBE, JP), suggested naming the Parkside Estate after London Boroughs. This seemed particularly appropriate, as the Tithe Farm Estate had been built to house the London Overspill, and the social housing on Parkside was built by the Greater London Council.

The names Chelsea, Hammersmith, Bromley, Finsbury, Bloomsbury and Kensington were all named as possible suggestions, and were to be called either Drive or Close. However when the final decision was made, Luton and Rural District Council preferred the name 'Gardens', rather than the Houghton Regis Parish Council's suggestions, and so the roads in that particular phase of development, became known in the majority as, 'Gardens'. All of the above names were adopted with the exception of 'Finsbury'. Kensington, which was used at a later stage elsewhere in the town. Incidentally, if you live in number 13, on any of the streets, on the Parkside Estate, you should actually count yourself lucky because many roads in the town were actually built without one!

BURFORD WALK	FAREHAM WAY	HINTON WALK
KIRTON WAY	LEASIDE	MELTON WALK

Left-
Hinton Walk
photographed in June
2015 (SEG).

There is no mention in the Council Minutes of 1972 about these street names, which were suggested by the builders M.J Shanley. It is noted that most of these are place names and it is possible, but by no means definite, that they have a connection with a Houghton, elsewhere.

There are, of course, many Houghton's dotted across the country, and town and villages which have similar 'features' to Houghton Regis. There might perhaps be an All Saints Church, or a perhaps a Village Green (or two!). Some of the above named streets (with the exception of Melton and Burford) all have churches named All Saints nearby or are near to another 'Houghton'. However the link to Houghton Regis, is, perhaps somewhat tenuous.

The only street which has a local link is Leaside. The name Luton is derived from the name 'Lea Town' (River Lea), and Leaside does face on to the vacant land bordering Luton. There is a brook, which runs under the ground beneath Park Road North and across to Parkside before heading into Luton, prior to heading towards Marsh Farm.

An aerial photograph taken on 22nd June 1981 showing the marking out for the Barratt's Estate. Photo reproduced with kind permission of Central Bedfordshire Council©.

The houses on Conway Close, Cumbria Close, Fensome Drive, Henley Close and Rosedale (1981) were built by the developers Barratt Homes. The Town Council was asked to suggest names for the whole estate, taking into account advice from the builders themselves. It is believed that all of the roads were named after the property types that they were building (as in 'The Cumbria').

CONQUEST ROAD

It is unfortunate, that there are no details in the council minute books about the reason behind the naming of many of the streets in the Parkside Estate. Conquest Road was named following a suggestion made by builders M.J Shanley.

It looks possible, that many of the surrounding streets to Conquest Road were decided upon due to the connection with a place nearby called 'Houghton'. There is a place called Houghton Conquest, which is located along the A6 towards Bedford. In common with other place names on the Parkside Estate, Houghton Conquest has a church called 'All Saints'.

DOLPHIN DRIVE | NEPTUNE SQUARE | TRIDENT DRIVE

Neptune, the Roman God of the Sea carried a Trident, which had three prongs and rode on a Dolphin or a horse. Although these is no apparent reason why the roads were named after Roman Mythology, a glance, at the map of Parkside Drive, reveals that Trident Drive is in three 'pronged' sections. This may provide the reason for these names.

DYLAN COURT

There is very little known about the naming of Dylan Court! Suggestions from the Council Minutes, show entries for 'North Park Court' and 'South Park Court' (one of which would be for Dylan Court, and the other for Manning Court). The most notable Dylan in recent history is the Welsh poet Dylan Thomas, but the name also relates to the Celtic God of the Sea.

ELM PARK CLOSE

Left-
Elm Park Close
pictured in June
2015 (SEG).

As with its neighbours, Elm Park Close was named after an area in London. Elm Park is a suburban district in East London, and falls within the Borough of Havering.

ENFIELD CLOSE

Above-
A show home photographed in 1972. Picture reproduced by kind permission of the London Metropolitan Archives, City of London (ref: 243770 collage.cityoflondon.gov.uk).

Most of the streets on the Parkside Estate were named after London Boroughs, to commemorate the fact that the first houses on the estate were built for the London Overspill.

The picture on above is of the sitting room, in a show home in Enfield Close taken in 1972. The house shows bright modern décor, and the estate featured plenty of green areas of open space between the streets.

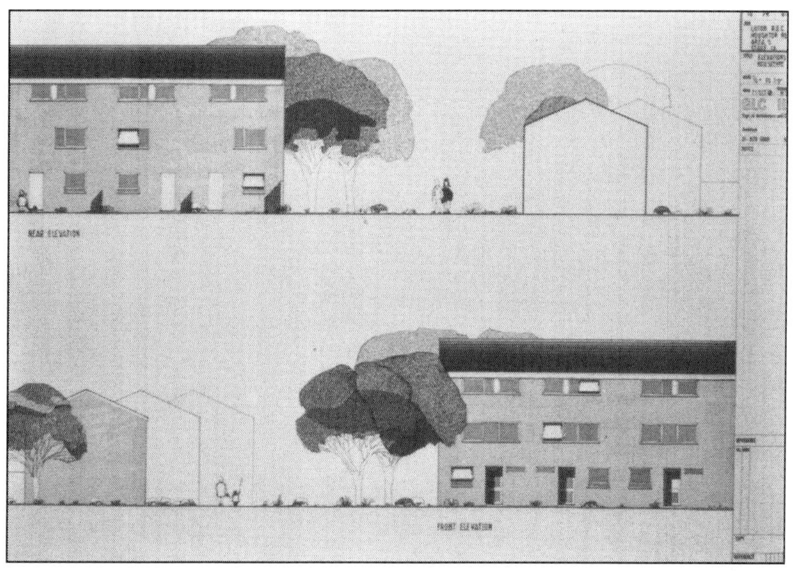

Above-
Architects plans for houses the three storey houses in Enfield Close. Picture reproduced by kind permission of the London Metropolitan Archives, City of London (ref: 243749 collage.cityoflondon.gov.uk).

FENWICK ROAD

The original suggestion for Fenwick Road (1975) was Franklin Road. However the name already existed in Dunstable, and members of the Parish Council were concerned that this may result in some confusion. Fenwick Road was suggested instead. It is known that Franklin was the surname of a one time owner of Chantry Farm, which is from where the original suggestion may have arisen. Alternatively Franklin or Fenwick could have been a surname of a member of staff from M.J Shanley.

GILLIAN WAY

It is believed that Gillian Way might have been named after one of the ladies who worked for the company M.J Shanley, in line with the idea of naming some of the streets after employees.

GRANGEWAY | PARKWAY | ROSEWALK

Grangeway, Parkway and Rosewalk were suggested by M.J Shanley in 1971, who built the Houghton Park Estate. The majority of the names that were suggested to the Parish Council were accepted for this estate, except for 'Kingsway', which was potentially either Grangeway or Parkway. This was due to a road in Dunstable with the same name. It has been suggested that Rosewalk could have been named after a Rosie, who worked for the company or connected business.

HAMMERSMITH CLOSE

The area now occupied by Hammersmith Close, was the location of the former South Bedfordshire District Council Offices (and prior to that, Luton and Rural District Council). The building was demolished during the 1980s, after the new offices in High Street, North, Dunstable were built.

The South Bedfordshire District Council Area Cash Office, moved to the Town Council Offices in Peel Street, where it remained until 2006. It was agreed to name the street, Hammersmith Close for continuity purposes

HAMMERSMITH GARDENS

Left-
The stone laying ceremony at Houghton Regis Baptist Church on Hammersmith Gardens in 1974. Photo reproduced by kind permission of Keith Wallis.

Hammersmith Gardens (also named after a London Borough) is home to properties, as well as Houghton Regis Baptist Church (opened 1975), St Vincent's Roman Catholic Church, School and Social Club.

The Baptist Church was once located on the High Street, Houghton Regis, but it was demolished in about 1970. The new church opened in 1975 and as well as a place for worship, is also a venue for the local groups, which include the Community Link Project, the Singing Café, Rainbows and Brownies.

Left- Members of Houghton Regis Baptist Church at the stone laying ceremony in 1974. Photo reproduced by kind thanks to Keith Wallis.

Left- The inside of the Baptist Church, pictured in 2013 (SEG).

St Vincent's Church and Social Club are also situated on Hammersmith Gardens, (which replaced the original facilities on Tithe Farm Road). There is also a Primary School (St Vincent's Catholic Primary School), which was built and opened during the 1970s.

In 2008, the School added an extension to cater for additional pupils and this was called the 'Chris Carey Block' (named after Councillor Chris Carey, who was Town Mayor of Houghton Regis from 2006-2007). Councillor Carey was actively involved in St Vincent's, having served on the Board of Governors.

Left-
The plaque outside the 'Chris Carey Block' at St Vincent's Catholic Primary School, pictured at its opening on 24th September 2008. (SEG).

St Vincent's Social Club is a popular venue for all types of events, including Wedding Receptions, Christenings Coffee Mornings, and fundraising events. It has been used ,many times in the past, to host the Town Mayor of Houghton Regis' Civic Receptions.

Left-
Councillor Laura Ellaway (Town Mayor) with fellow guests, including the High Sheriff of Bedfordshire, Colin Osborne, MBE, and Mrs. Diane Osborne, the Mayor of Luton, Councillor Mohammed Farooq, Central Bedfordshire Councillor, Mrs. Susan Goodchild and the Mayor and Mayoress of Dunstable, Councillor and Mrs. Stock, at a charity Coffee Morning in March 2015 held by the Mayor of Houghton Regis at St Vincent's Social Club (SEG).

HOUGHTON PARK ROAD

MAPLE WAY

Houghton Park was the estate name for the private development built by M.J Shanley. Houghton Park Road is the name for the main service road which runs through the centre of the development. Maple Way is another service road which runs through the estate, and it is possible that the name comes from trees, which were planted in the area by the developers.

JOHNSON COURT

Left-
Johnson Court complex, taken June 2010 (SEG).

Johnson Court (1978) is a mystery – it is official! The properties were built by the Royal British Legion Housing Authority, and the minute book records that the flats were due to be named 'Arnold Court', after Mr. E.D Arnold MBE, BEM, who was Chairman of the County Association. This however never happened and there is no further reference to this. The complex was bought by Housing 21, in the 1980s, and is still managed and maintained by the group.

LINMERE WALK

Above-
Rosewalk in 1972. Photo reproduced by kind permission of the London Metropolitan Archives, City of London (ref: 243813 collage.cityoflondon.gov.uk).

The original suggestion for Linmere Walk (1971), made by builders M.J Shanley, was 'School Walk'. However this name was objected to and the name Linmere Walk was suggested by the Parish Council. It is also noted that there was already a School Walk in Tithe Farm. It would seem logical that it was a literal name as the road backed on to Linmear School (now called Kings Houghton Middle School), although it is noted that they are spelt differently.

There is a Long Linmere Furlong and Short Linmere Furlong on the Duke of Bedford's 1762 Map of Houghton Regis in the approximate area. Therefore the names have probably come from original furlong names.

LONGMEADOW

Unfortunately, the reason for this road name from 1975, has not been recorded, but it may just be a literal term. Nowadays, it seems unlikely that this name would be permitted owing to its similarity to both Long Mead, and Longmeadow, in Dunstable.

MANNING COURT

Left-
Manning Court, pictured in April 2015 (SEG).

'Manning Woods' were located behind the original Brookfields Avenue, and it is believed that Manning was the name of the farmer from Poynters Farm, in this area. Although there is no mention anywhere, on any records, about the reason for the street name, bearing in mind the location, it would seem likely that the two are related.

PARKSIDE DRIVE

Parkside Drive is the main street, which runs through the estate. For many years, the Carnival used to leave from the Parkside Drive Recreation Ground (often called 'the Dog and Duck') after the pub on the adjacent land. The Carnival procession was moved in 2011, just around the corner, and now starts from Houghton Regis Academy (formerly known as Kings Houghton Middle School).

Left - Councillor and Mrs Carey in the Carnival Procession in 2006. Photo reproduced by kind permission of Houghton Regis Town Council.

Left - The Town Council Tractor with a Jazz Band in the trailer, pictured at the 2009 Carnival. Photo reproduced by kind permission of Houghton Regis Town Council.

PLATZ HOUSE

Above left-
Left-Councillor Maurice Platz 1988 reproduced by kind permission of Bruce Turvey.
Above right-
Platz House pictured in April 2015 (SEG).

Platz House was named after Councillor Maurice Platz, who was both Chairman of the Parish Council between 1977 and 1979, and Mayor of the town in 1986/1987.

Councillor Platz passed away some years ago, but a trophy for the Houghton Regis Carnival was named in his honour, and the Maurice Platz Trophies were given to the Carnival Queen and Princess when were crowned.

WESTMINSTER GARDENS

Westminster Gardens was one of the last phases of houses to be built on Parkside, and features 'Scandinavian' style houses!

The street was named to fit in with the surrounding roads.

THE FUTURE

This book has looked back at the last century in Houghton Regis, but predominantly, the last 60 years. The town is moving towards change once more, and at the time of writing, new road networks were being created and housing developments planned. The future will bring new schools, retail and leisure facilities, employment, and many new opportunities.

The next 50 years will be another crucial time in the development of the town, and in the next century, it is certain that there will be much interest in this period. Much has changed about the way that developments and communities are built, and whatever the future holds, it is important that the past is not forgotten, nor the people who have been part of, and remain, 'Up Above The Streets and Houses'.

Above-
Views from the tower of All Saints Parish Church, May 2015 (SEG).

HOUGHTON SCENES

Above-
Trees on the Village Green under snow! February 2012 (SEG).

Above-
Bedford Square Shopping Centre 2009. Photo reproduced by kind permission of Houghton Regis Town Council.

Left-
The Memorial Stone, 2002 (SEG).

STREET INDEX

STREET INDEX

STREET INDEX

ABOUT THE AUTHOR

Sarah Gelsthorp was born in Luton, Bedfordshire in 1977, and apart from spending four years living in Newquay, Cornwall, has remained living only six miles away from her childhood home, residing in Dunstable. Sarah has worked for Houghton Regis Town Council since 2002, as the Town Mayor's Secretary/Promotions and Communications Officer, and has written many publications for print, including the Houghton Regis Town Guides from 2005-2012 and the Town Crier Newsletter from 2004-2014. In addition, Sarah organises the annual Town Carnival and public events for the council.

Sarah is married with one daughter.

ACKNOWLEDGEMENTS

I have been so fortunate with the amount of support that I have received with the collation of this book, and I am grateful to each and every person who has helped me with research, photographs, and with giving me their time.

I would like to particularly like to thank Ashwell Parish Council, John Buckledee, Tom Burnham, Pamela Cameron, Daphne Carey, Irene Carpenter, James Carroll, Central Bedfordshire Council, Jean Cheshire, Stephen Coleman, Maria Cooper Janis, Geoff Cox, Andrew Duerden, Dunstable Gazette, Jenny and Eric Gallucci, John Gelsthorp, Shirley Gilchrist, Richard Goosey, Jon Green, Diane Hall, Bob Harrington, Justin Hawkins, Tony Hemmings, David Hill, Robin Hines, Houghton Regis Back In The Day members on Facebook, Houghton Regis Heritage Society, Houghton Regis News Desk (Facebook), Houghton Regis Police, Houghton Regis Women's Institute, Beverly Lennox, London Metropolitan Archives, Jane Lousada, Pat Lovering, Luton News, Mead Estates Ltd, Theresa Pritchett, Roger Marsh & Co, Mary Sidgwick, Chris and Susan Slough, Jeremy Smith, Dudley Smy, Peter Stanton, Marilyn Tommey, Bruce Turvey, Trevor Turvey, David Underwood, 'Up Above The Streets and Houses' friends on Facebook, Keith Wallis, Linda Wilson and Vauxhall Motors.

I would also like to give a special thanks to my colleagues at Houghton Regis Town Council, for their unfailing support with this project.

Sarah Gelsthorp